THE ELEMENTS OF GENERAL METHOD, BASED ON THE PRINCIPLES OF HERBART

First published 1893
This edition published by Lector House in 2024

ISBN: 978-93-6138-765-4

Lector House LLP
Registered Office: H. No. 96, Block C, Tomar Colony,
Burari, Delhi – 110084, India
info@lectorhouse.com
www.lectorhouse.com

THE ELEMENTS OF GENERAL METHOD, BASED ON THE PRINCIPLES OF HERBART

CHARLES ALEXANDER MCMURRY

2024

LECTOR HOUSE LLP

THE ELEMENTS OF GENERAL METHOD, BASED ON THE PRINCIPLES OF HERBART.

BY

CHARLES A. MCMURRY, PH.D.

SECOND EDITION

PREFACE.

The Herbart School of Pedagogy has created much stir in Germany in the last thirty years. It has developed a large number of vigorous writers on all phases of education and psychology, and numbers a thousand or more positive disciples among the energetic teachers of Germany.

Those American teachers and students who have come in contact with the ideas of this school have been greatly stimulated.

In such a miscellaneous and many-sided thing as practical education, it is deeply gratifying to find a clear and definite leading purpose that prevails throughout and a set of mutually related and supporting principles which in practice contribute to the realization of this purpose.

The following chapters cannot be regarded as a full, exact, and painfully scientific account of Herbartian ideas, but as a simple explanation of their leading principles in their relations to each other and in their application to our own school problems.

In the second edition the last chapter of the first edition has been omitted, while the other chapters have been much modified and enlarged. The chapter on the Formal Steps is reserved for enlargement and publication in a separate form.

NORMAL, ILL., November 4, 1893.

CONTENTS

CHAPTER I.

THE CHIEF AIM OF EDUCATION.

What is the central purpose of education? If we include under this term all the things commonly assigned to it, its many phases as represented by the great variety of teachers and pupils, the many branches of knowledge and the various and even conflicting methods in bringing up children, it is difficult to find a definition sufficiently broad and definite to compass its meaning. In fact we shall not attempt in the beginning to make a definition. We are in search not so much of a comprehensive definition as of a central truth, a key to the situation, an aim that will simplify and brighten all the work of teachers. Keeping in view the end from the beginning, we need a central organizing principle which shall dictate for teacher and pupil the highway over which they shall travel together.

We will assume at least that education means the whole bringing up of a child from infancy to maturity, not simply his school training. The reason for this assumption is that home, school, companions, environment, and natural endowment, working through a series of years, produce a character which is a unit as the resultant of these different influences and growths. Again, we are compelled to assume that this aim, whatever it is, is the same for all.

Now what will the average man, picked up at random, say to our question: What is the chief end in the education of your son? A farmer wishes his boy to read, write, and cipher, so as to meet successfully the needs of a farmer's life. The merchant desires that his boy get a wider reach of knowledge and experience so as to succeed in a livelier sort of business competition. A university professor would lay out a liberal course of training for his son so as to prepare him for intellectual pursuits among scholars and people of culture. This utilitarian view, which points to success in life in the ordinary sense, is the prevailing one. We could probably sum up the wishes of a great majority of the common people by saying, "They desire to give their children, through education, a better chance in life than they themselves have had." Yet even these people, if pressed to give reasons, would admit that the purely utilitarian view is a low one and that there is something better for every boy and girl than the mere ability to make a successful living.

Turn for a moment to the great *systems* of education which have held their own for centuries and examine their aims. The Jesuits, the Humanists, and the Natural Scientists all claimed to be liberal, culture-giving, and preparatory to great things; yet we only need to quote from the histories of education to show their narrowness and incompleteness. The training of the Jesuits was linguistic and rhetorical, and almost entirely apart from our present notion of human development. The Humanists or Classicists who for so many centuries constituted the educational elite, belonged to the past with its glories rather than to the age in which they really lived. Though standing in a modern age, they were almost blind to the great problems and opportunities it offered. They stood in bold contrast to the growth of the modern spirit in history, literature, and natural science. But in spite of their predominating influence over education for centuries, there has never been the shadow of a chance for making the classics of antiquity the basis of common, popular education. The modern school of Natural Scientists is just as one-sided as the Humanists in supposing that human nature is narrow enough to be compressed within the bounds of natural science studies, however broad their field may be.

But the systems of education in vogue have always lagged behind the clear views of educational *reformers*. Two hundred fifty years ago Comenius projected a plan of education for every boy and girl of the common people. His aim was to teach all men all things from the highest truths of religion to the commonest things of daily experience. Being a man of simple and profound religious faith, religion and morality were at the foundation of his system. But even the principles of intellectual training so clearly advocated by Comenius have not yet found a ready hearing among teachers, to say nothing of his great moral-religious purpose. Among later writers, Locke, Rousseau, and Pestalozzi have set up ideals of education that have had much influence. But Locke's "gentleman" can never be the ideal of all because it is intrinsically aristocratic and education has become with us broadly democratic. After all, Locke's "gentleman" is a noble ideal and should powerfully impress teachers. The perfect human animal that Rousseau dreamed of in the Emile, is best illustrated in the noble savage, but we are not in danger in America of adopting this ideal. In spite of his merits the noblest savage falls short in several ways. Yet it is important in education to perfect the physical powers and the animal development in every child. Pestalozzi touched the hearts of even the weakest and morally frailest children, and tried to make improved physical conditions and intellectual culture contribute to heart culture, or rather to combine the two in strong moral character. He came close upon the highest aim of education and was able to illustrate his doctrine in practice. The educational reformers have gone far ahead of the schoolmasters in setting up a high aim in education.

Let us examine a few well-known definitions of education by great thinkers, and try to discover a central idea.

"The purpose of education is to give to the body and to the soul all the beauty and all the perfection of which they are capable."—*Plato.*

"Education includes whatever we do for ourselves and whatever is done for us by others for the express purpose of bringing us nearer to the perfection of our nature."—*John Stuart Mill.*

"Education is the preparation for complete living."—*Herbert Spencer.*

"Education is the harmonious and equable evolution of the human faculties by a method based upon the nature of the mind for developing all the faculties of the soul, for stirring up and nourishing all the principles of life, while shunning all one-sided culture and taking account of the sentiments upon which the strength and worth of men depend." —*Stein*.

"Education is the sum of the reflective efforts by which we aid nature in the development of the physical, intellectual, and moral faculties of man in view of his perfection, his happiness, and his social destination." —*Compayre*.

These attempts to bring the task of education into a comprehensive, scientific formula are interesting and yet disappointing. They agree in giving great breadth to education. But in the attempt to be comprehensive, to omit nothing, they fail to specify that wherein the *true worth* of man consists; they fail to bring out into relief the highest aim as an organizing idea in the complicated work of education and its relation to secondary aims.

We desire therefore to approach nearer to this problem: *What is the highest aim of education*?

We will do so by an inquiry into the aims and tendencies of our public schools. To an outward observer the schools of today confine their attention almost exclusively to the acquisition of certain forms of knowledge and to intellectual training, to the mental discipline and power that come from a varied and vigorous exercise of the faculties. The great majority of good schoolmasters stand squarely upon this platform, knowledge and mental discipline. But they are none the less deeply conscious that this is not the highest aim of education. We scarcely need to be told that a person may be fully equipped with the best that this style of education can give, and still remain a criminal. A good and wise parent will inevitably seek for a better result in his child than mere knowledge, intellectual ability, and power. All good schoolmasters know that behind school studies and cares is the still greater task of developing manly and womanly character. Perhaps, however, this is too high and sacred a thing to formulate. Perhaps in the attempt to reduce it to a scientific form we should lose its spirit. Admitting that strong moral character is the noblest result of right training, is it not still incidental to the regular school work? Perhaps it lies in the teacher and in his manner of teaching subjects, and not in the subject-matter itself nor in any course of study.

This is exactly the point at which we wish to apply the lever and to lift into prominence the *moral character-building aim* as the central one in education. This aim should be like a loadstone, attracting and subordinating all other purposes to itself. It should dominate in the choice, arrangement, and method of studies.

Let us examine more carefully the convictions upon which the moral aim rests. Every wise and benevolent parent knows that the first and last question to ask and answer regarding a child is "What are his moral quality and strength?" Now, who is better able to judge of the true aim than thoughtful and solicitous *parents*? In the second place, it is inconceivable that a conscientious *teacher* should close his eyes to all except the intellectual training of his pupils. It is as natural for him to touch and awaken the moral qualities as it is for birds to sing. Again, the *state* is more concerned to see the growth of just and virtuous citizens than in seeing the prosperity of scholars, inventors, and merchants. It is also concerned with the success of the latter, but chiefly when their knowledge, skill, and wealth are equaled by their virtues. Our country may have vast resources and great opportunities, but everything in the end depends upon the *moral quality* of its men and women. Undermine and corrupt this and we all know that there is nothing to hope for. The uncorrupted stock of true patriots in our land is firmly rooted in this conviction, which is worth more to the country than corn-fields and iron mines. The perpetual enticement and blandishment of worldly success so universal in our time can not move us if we found one theory and practice upon the central doctrine of moral education. Education, therefore, in its popular, untrammeled, moral sense, is the greatest concern of society.

In projecting a general plan of popular education we are beholden to the prejudices of no man nor class of men. Not even the traditional prejudices of the great body of teachers should stand in the way of setting up the noblest ideal of education. Educational thinkers are in duty bound to free themselves from utilitarian notions and narrowness, and to adopt the best platform that children by natural birthright can stand upon. They are called upon to find the best and to apply it to as many as possible. Let it be remembered that each child has a complete growth before him. His own possibilities and not the attainments of his parents and elders are the things to consider.

Shall we seek to avoid responsibility for the moral aim by throwing it upon the family and the church? But the more we probe into educational problems the more we shall find the essential unity of all educational forces. The citadel of a child's life is his moral character, whether the home, the school, or the church build and strengthen its walls. If asked to define the relation of the school to the home we shall quickly see that they are one in spirit and leading purpose, that instead of being separated they should be brought closer together.

In conclusion, therefore, shall we make *moral character* the clear and conscious aim of school education, and then subordinate school studies and discipline, mental training and conduct, to this aim? It will be a great stimulus to thousands of teachers to discover that this is the real purpose of school work, and that there are abundant means not yet used of realizing it. Having once firmly grasped this idea, they will find that there is no other having half its potency. It will put a substantial foundation under educational labors, both theoretical and practical, which will make them the noblest of enterprises. Can we expect the public school to drop into such a purely subordinate function as that of intellectual training; to limit its influence to an almost mechanical action, the sharpening of the mental tools? Stated in this form, it becomes an absurdity.

Is it reasonable to suppose that the rank and file of our teachers will realize the importance of this aim in teaching so long as it has no recognition in our public system of instruction? The moral element is largely present among educators as an *instinct*, but it ought to be evolved into a *clear purpose* with definite means of accomplishment. It is an open secret in fact, that while our public instruction is ostensibly secular, having nothing to do directly with religion or morals, there is nothing about which good teachers are more thoughtful and anxious than about the means of moral influence. Occasionally some one from the outside attacks our public schools as without morals and godless, but there is no lack of staunch defenders on moral grounds. Theoretically and even practically, to a considerable extent, we are all agreed upon the great value of moral education. But there is a striking inconsistency in our whole position on the school problem. While the supreme value of the moral aim will be generally admitted, it has no open recognition in our school course, either as a principal or as a subordinate aim of instruction. Moral education is not germane to the avowed purposes of the public school. If it gets in at all it is by the back door. It is incidental, not primary. The importance of making the leading aim of education clear and *conscious* to teachers, is great. If their conviction on this point is not clear they will certainly not concentrate their attention and efforts upon its realization. Again, in a business like education, where there are so many important and necessary results to be reached, it is very easy and common to put forward a subordinate aim, and to lift it into undue prominence, even allowing it to swallow up all the energies of teacher and pupils. Owing to this diversity of opinion among teachers as to the results to be reached, our public schools exhibit a chaos of conflicting theory and practice, and a numberless brood of hobby-riders.

How to establish the moral aim in the center of the school course, how to subordinate and realize the other educational aims while keeping this chiefly in view, how to make instruction and school discipline contribute unitedly to the formation of vigorous moral character, and how to unite home, school, and other life experiences of a child in perfecting the one great aim of education—these are some of the problems whose solution will be sought in the following chapters.

It will be especially our purpose to show how *school instruction* can be brought into the direct service of character-building. This is the point upon which most teachers are skeptical. Not much effort has been made of late to put the best moral materials into the school course. In one whole set of school studies, and that the most important (reading, literature, and history), there is opportunity through all the grades for a vivid and direct cultivation of moral ideas and convictions. The second great series of studies, the natural sciences, come in to support the moral aims, while the personal example and influence of the teacher, and the common experiences and incidents of school life and conduct, give abundant occasion to apply and enforce moral ideas.

That the other justifiable aims of education, such as physical training, mental discipline, orderly habits, gentlemanly conduct, practical utility of knowledge, liberal culture, and the free development of individuality will not be weakened by placing the moral aim in the forefront of educational motives, we are convinced. To some extent these questions will be discussed in the following pages.

CHAPTER II.

RELATIVE VALUE OF STUDIES.

Being convinced that the controlling aim of education should be moral, we shall now inquire into the relative value of different studies and their fitness to reach and satisfy this aim. As measured upon this cardinal purpose, what is the intrinsic value of each school study? The branches of knowledge furnish the materials upon which a child's mind works. Before entering upon such a long and up-hill task as education, with its weighty results, it is prudent to estimate not only the end in view, but the best means of reaching it. Many means are offered, some trivial, others valuable. A careful measurement, with some reliable standard, of the materials furnished by the common school, is our first task. To what extent does history contribute to our purpose? What importance have geography and arithmetic? How do reading and natural science aid a child to grow into the full stature of a man or woman?

These questions are not new, but the answer to them has been long delayed. Since the time of Comenius, to say the least, they have seriously disturbed educators. But few have had the courage, industry, and breadth of mind of a Comenius, to sound the educational waters and to lay out a profitable chart. In spite of Comenius' labors, however, and those of other educational reformers be they never so energetic, practical progress toward a final answer, as registered in school courses, has been extremely slow.

Herbert Spencer says: "If there needs any further evidence of the rude, undeveloped character of our education, we have it in the fact that the comparative worths of the different kinds of knowledge have been as yet scarcely even discussed, much less discussed in a methodic way with definite results. Not only is it that no standard of relative values has yet been agreed upon, but the existence of any such standard has not been conceived in any clear manner. And not only is it that the existence of such a standard has not been clearly conceived, but the need of it seems to have been scarcely even felt. Men read books on this topic and attend lectures upon that, decide that their children shall be instructed in these branches and not in those; and all under the guidance of mere custom, or liking, or prejudice, without ever considering the enormous importance of determining in some rational way what things are really most worth learning. * * * * * Men dress their children's minds as they do their bodies, in the prevailing fashion." Spencer, *Education*, p. 26.

Spencer sees clearly the importance of this problem and gives it a vigorous discussion in his first chapter, "What knowledge is of most worth?" But the question is a broad and fundamental one and in his preference for the natural sciences he seems to us not to have maintained a just balance of educational forces in preparing a child for "complete living." His theory needs also to be worked out into greater detail and applied to school conditions before it can be of much value to teachers. It can scarcely be said that any other Englishman or American has seriously grappled with this problem. Great changes and reforms indeed have been started, especially within the last fifty years, but they have been undertaken under the pressure of general popular demands and have resulted in compromises between traditional forces and urgent popular needs. An adequate philosophical inquiry into the relative merit of studies and their adaptability to nurture mental, moral, and physical qualities has not been made.

The Germans have worked to a better purpose. Quite a number of able thinkers among them have given their best years to the study of this problem of relative educational values and to a working out of its results. Herbart, Ziller, Stoy, and Rein have been deeply interested in philosophy and psychology as life-long teachers of these subjects at the university, but in their practice schools in the same place they also stood daily face to face with the primary difficulties of ordinary teaching. At the outset, and before laying out a course of study, they were compelled to meet and settle the aim of education and the problem of relative values. Having answered these questions to their own satisfaction, they proceeded to work out in detail a common school course. The Herbart school of teachers has presumed to call its interpretation of educational ideas "scientific pedagogy," a somewhat pretentious name in view of the fact that many leading educators in Germany, England, and elsewhere, deny the existence of such a science. But if not a science, it is at least a serious attempt at one. The exposition of principles that follow is chiefly derived from them.

With us the present time is favorable to a rational inquiry into relative educational values and to a thorough-going application of the results to school courses and methods.

In the first place the old *classical monopoly* is finally and completely broken, at least so far as the common school is concerned. It ruled education for several centuries, but now even its methods of discipline are losing their antique hold. The natural sciences, modern history, and literature have assumed an equal place with the old classical studies in college courses. Freed from old traditions and prejudice, our common school is now grounded in the vernacular, in the national history and literature, and in home geography and natural science. Its roots go deep into native soil. *Secondly*, the door of the common school has been thrown open to the new studies and they have entered in a troop. History, drawing, natural science, modern literature, and physical culture have been added to the old reading, writing, and arithmetic. The common school was never so untrammeled. It is free to absorb into its course the select materials of the best studies. Teachers really enjoy more freedom in selecting and arranging subjects and in introducing new things than they know how to make use of. There is no one in high authority to check the reform spirit and even local boards are often among the advocates of change. *In the third place,* by multiplying studies, the common school course has grown more complex and heterogeneous. The old reading, writing, arithmetic, and grammar could not be shelved for the sake of the new studies and the same amount of time must be divided now among many branches. It is not to be wondered at if all the studies are treated in a shallow and fragmentary way. Some of the new studies, especially, are not well taught. There is less of unity in higher education now than there was before the classical studies and "the three R's" lost their supremacy. Our common school course has become a batch of miscellanies. We are in danger of overloading pupils, as well as of making a superficial hodge-podge of all branches. There is imperative need for sifting the studies according to their value, as well as for bringing them into right connection and dependence upon one another. *Fourthly,* there is a large body of thoughtful and inquiring teachers and principals who are working at a revision of the school course. They seek something tangible, a working plan, which will help them in their present perplexities and show them a wise use of drawing, natural science, and literature, in harmony with the other studies. *Finally,* since we are in the midst of such a breaking-up period, we need to take our bearings. In order to avoid mistakes and excesses there is a call for deep, impartial, and many-sided thinking on educational problems. Supposing that we know what the controlling aim of education is, we are next led to inquire about and to determine the relative value of studies as tributary to this aim.

It is not however our purpose to give an original solution to this problem and to those which follow it. We must decline to attempt a philosophical inquiry into fundamental principles and their origin. Ours is the humbler task of explaining and applying principles already worked out by others; that is, to give the results of Herbartian pedagogy as applied to our schools.

Instead of discussing the many branches of study one after another, it will be well to make a broad division of them into three classes and observe the marked features and value of each. First, *history,* including the subject matter of biography, history, story, and other parts of literature. Second, the *natural sciences.* Third, *the formal studies,* grammar, writing, much of arithmetic, and the symbols used in reading.

The first two open up the great fields of real knowledge and experience, the world of man and of external nature, the two great reservoirs of interesting facts. We will first examine these two fields and consider their value as constituent parts of the school course.

History, in our present sense, includes what we usually understand by it, as U. S. history, modern and ancient history, also biography, tradition, fiction as expressing human life and the novel or romance, and historical and literary masterpieces of all sorts, as the drama and the epic poem, so far as they delineate man's experience and character. In a still broader sense, history includes language as the expression of men's thoughts and feelings. But this is the formal side of history with which we are not at present concerned. History deals with men's motives and actions as individuals or in society, with their dispositions, habits, and institutions, and with the monuments and literature they have left.

The relations of persons to each other in society give rise to morals. How? The act of a person—as when a fireman rescues a child from a burning building—shows a disposition in the actor. We praise or condemn this disposition as the deed is good or bad. But each moral judgment, rightly given, leaves us stronger. To appreciate and judge fairly the life and acts of a woman like Mary Lyon, or of a man such as Samuel Armstrong, is to awaken something of their spirit and moral temper in ourselves. Whether in the life of David or of Shylock, or of the people whom they represent, the study of men is primarily a study of morals, of conduct. It is in the personal hardships, struggles, and mutual contact of men that motives and moral impulses are observed and weighed. In such men as John Bunyan, William the Silent, and John Quincy Adams, we are much interested to know what qualities of mind and heart they possessed, and especially what human sympathies and antipathies they felt. Livingstone embodied in his African life certain Christian virtues which we love and honor the more because they were so severely and successfully tested. Although the history of men and of society has many uses, its best influence is in illustrating and inculcating moral ideas. It is teaching morals by example. Even living companions often exert less influence upon children than the characters impressed upon their minds from reading. The deliberate plan of teachers and parents might make this influence more salutary and effective.

It will strike most teachers as a surprise to say that *the chief use of history study is to form moral notions in children*. Their experience with this branch of school work has been quite different. They have not so regarded nor used history. It has been generally looked upon as a body of useful information that intelligent persons must possess. Our history texts also have been constructed for another purpose, namely, to summarize and present important facts in as brief space as possible, not to reveal personal actions and character as a formative moral influence in the education of the young. Even as sources of valuable information, Spencer shows that our histories have been extremely deficient; but for moral purposes they are almost worthless.

Now, moral dispositions are a better fruitage and test of worth in men than any intellectual acquirements. History is already a recognized study of admitted value in the schools. It is a shame to strip it of that content and of that influence which are its chief merit. To study the conduct of persons as illustrating right actions is, in quality, the highest form of instruction. Other very important things are also involved in a right study of history. There are economic, political, and social institutions evolved out of previous history; there are present intricate problems to be approached and understood. But all these questions rest to a large extent upon moral principles. But while these political, social, and economic interests are beyond the present reach of children, biography, individual life and action in their simple forms, are plain to their understanding. They not only make moral conduct real and impressive, but they gradually lead up to an appreciation of history in its social and institutional forms.

Some of the best historical materials (from biography, tradition, and fiction) should be absorbed by children in each grade as an essential part of the substratum of moral ideas. This implies more than a collection of historical stories in a supplementary reader for intermediate grades. It means that history in the broad sense is to be an important study in every grade, and that it shall become a center and reservoir from which reading books and language lessons draw their supplies. These biographies, stories, and historical episodes must be the best which our history and classic literature can furnish, and whatever is of like virtue in the life of other kindred peoples, of England, Germany, Greece, etc.

If history in this sense can be made a strong auxiliary to moral education in common schools, the whole body of earnest teachers will be gratified. For there is no theme among them of such perennial interest and depth of meaning as *moral culture* in schools. It is useless to talk of confining our teachers to the intellectual exercises outlined in text books. They are conscious of dealing with children of moral susceptibility. In our meetings, discussions on the means of moral influence are more frequent and earnest than on any other topic; and in their daily work hundreds of our teachers are aiming at moral character in children more than at anything else. As they free themselves from mechanical requirements and begin to recognize their true function, they discover the transcendent importance of moral education, that it underlies and gives meaning to all the other work of the teacher.

But teachers heretofore have taken a narrow view of the moral influences at their disposal. Their ever-recurring emphatic refrain has been "*the example of the teacher,*" and, to tell the truth, there is no better means of instilling moral ideas than the presence and inspiration of a high-toned teacher. We know, however, that teachers need moral stimulus and encouragement as much as anybody. It will not do to suppose that they have reached the pinnacle of moral excellence and can stand as all-sufficient exemplars to children. The teacher himself must have food as well as the children. He must partake of the loaf he distributes to them. The clergyman also should be an example of Christian virtue, but he preaches the gospel as illustrated in the life of Christ, of St. Paul, and of others. In pressing home moral and religious truths his appeal is to great sources of inspiration which lie outside of himself. Why should the teacher rely upon his own unaided example more than the preacher? No teacher can feel that he embodies in himself, except in an imperfect way, the strong moral ideas that have made the history of good men worth reading. No matter what resources he may have in his own character, the teacher needs to employ moral forces that lie outside of himself, ideals toward which he struggles and towards which he inspires and leads others. The very fact that he appreciates and admires a man like Longfellow or Peter Cooper will stir the children with like feelings. In this sense it is a mistake to center all attention upon the conduct of the teacher. He is but a guide, or, like Goldsmith's preacher, he allures to brighter worlds and leads the way. It is better for pupil and teacher to enter into the companionship of common aims and ideals. For them to study together and admire the conduct of Roger Williams is to bring them into closer sympathy, and what do teachers need more than to get into *personal sympathy* with their children? Let them climb the hill together, and enjoy the views together, and grow so intimate in their aims and sympathies that afterlife cannot break the bond. When the inspirations and aims thus gained have gradually changed into tendencies and habits, the child is morally full-fledged. It is high ground upon which to land youth, or aid in landing him, but it is clearly in view.

It is only gradually that moral ideas gain an ascendency, first over the thoughts and feelings of a child and later still over his conduct. Many good impressions at first seem to bear no fruit in action. But examples and experience reiterate the truth till it finds a firm lodgment and begins to act as a check upon natural impulses. Many a child reads the stories in the *Youth's Companion* with absorbing interest but in the home circle fails noticeably to imitate the conduct he admires. But moral ideas must grow a little before they can yield fruit. The seed of example must drop into the soil of the mind under favorable conditions; it must germinate and send up its shoots to some height before its presence and nature can be clearly seen. The application of moral ideas to conduct is very important even in childhood, out patience and care are necessary in most cases. There must be timely sowing of the seed and judicious cultivation, if good fruits are to be gathered later on. There is indeed much anxiety and painful uncertainty on the part of those who charge themselves with the moral training of children. Labor and birth pains are antecedent to the delivery of a moral being. Then again a child must develop according to what is in him, his nature and peculiar disposition. The processes of growth are within him and the best you can do is to give them scope. He is *free* and you are *bound* to minister to his best freedom. The common school age is the *formative period*. At six a child is morally immature; at fifteen the die has been stamped. This youthful wilderness must be crossed. We can't turn back. There is no other way of reaching the promised land. But there are rebellions and haltings and disorderly scenes.

This is a tortuous road! Isn't there a quicker and easier way? The most speedily constructed road across this region is *a short treatise* on morals for teacher and pupil. In this way it is possible to have all the virtues and faults tabulated, labeled, and transferred in brief space to the minds of the children (if the discipline is rigorous enough). Swallow a catechism, reduced to a verbal memory product. Pack away the essence of morals in a few general laws and rules and have the children learn them. Some day they may understand. What astounding faith in memory cram and dry forms! We *can* pave such a road through the fields of moral science, but when a child has traveled it is he a whit the better? No such paved road is good for anything. It isn't even comfortable. It has been tried a dozen times in much less important fields of knowledge than morals. Moral ideas spring up out of experience with persons either in real life or in the books we read. Examples of moral action drawn from life are the only thing that can give meaning to moral precepts. If we see a harsh man beating his horse, we get an ineffaceable impression of harshness. By reading the story of the Black Beauty we acquire a lively sympathy for animals. Then the maxim "A merciful man is merciful to his beast" will be a good summary of the impressions received. Moral ideas always have a concrete basis or origin. Some companion with whose feelings and actions you are in close personal contact, or some character from history or fiction by whose personality you have been strongly attracted, gives you your keenest impressions of moral qualities. To begin with abstract moral teaching, or to put faith in it, is to misunderstand children. In morals as in other forms of knowledge, children are overwhelmingly interested in personal and individual examples, things which have form, color, action. The attempt to sum up the important truths of a subject and present them as abstractions to children is almost certain to be a failure, pedagogically considered. It has been demonstrated again and again, even in high schools, that botany, chemistry, physics, and zoology can not be taught by such brief scientific compendia of rules and principles—"Words, words, words," as Hamlet said. We can not learn geography from definitions and map questions, nor morals from catechisms. And just as in natural science we are resorting perforce to plants, animals, and natural phenomena, so in morals we turn to the deeds and lives of men. Columbus in his varying fortunes leaves vivid impressions of the moral strength and weakness of himself and of others. John Winthrop gives frequent examples of generous and unselfish good-will to the settlers about Boston. Little Lord Fauntleroy is a better treatise on morals for children than any of our sermonizers have written. We must get at morals without moralizing and drink in moral convictions without resorting to moral platitudes. Educators are losing faith in words, definitions, and classifications. It is a truism that we can't learn chemistry or zoology from books alone, nor can moral judgments be rendered except from individual actions.

A little reflection will show that we are only demanding *object lessons* in the field of moral education, extensive, systematic object lessons; choice experiences and episodes from human life, simple and clear, painted in natural colors, as shown by our best history and literature. To appreciate the virtues and vices, to sympathize with better impulses, we must travel beyond words and definitions till we come in contact with the personal deeds that first give rise to them. The life of Martin Luther, with its faults and merits honestly represented, is a powerful moral tonic to the reader; the autobiography of Franklin brings out a great variety of homely truths in the form of interesting episodes in his career. Adam Bede and Romola impress us more powerfully and permanently than the best sermons, because the individual realism in them leads to a vividness of moral judgment of their acts unequalled. King Lear teaches us the folly of a rash judgment with overwhelming force. Evangeline awakens our sympathies as no moralist ever dreamed of doing. Uncle Tom in Mrs. Stowe's story was a stronger preacher than Wendell Phillips. William Tell in Schiller's play kindles our love for heroic deeds into an enthusiasm. The best myths, historical biographies, novels, and dramas, are the richest sources of moral stimulus because they lead us into the immediate presence of those men and women whose deeds stir up our moral natures. In the representations of the masters we are in the presence of moral ideas clothed in flesh and blood, real and yet idealized. Generosity is not a name but the act of a person which wins our interest and, favor. To get the impress of kindness we must see an act of kindness and feel the glow it produces. When Sir Philip Sidney, wounded on the battle field and suffering with thirst, reached out his hand for a cup of water that was brought, his glance fell upon a dying soldier who viewed the cup with great desire; Sidney handed him the water with the words, "Thy necessity is greater than mine." No one can refuse his approval for this act. After telling the story of the man who went down to Jericho and fell among thieves, and then of the priest, the Levite, and the Samaritan who passed that way, Jesus put the question to his critic, "Who was neighbor to him that fell among thieves?" And the answer came even from unwilling lips, "He that showed mercy." When Nathan Hale on the scaffold regretted that he had but one life to lose for his country, we realize better what patriotism is. On the other hand it is natural to *condemn wrong deeds* when presented clearly and objectively in the action of another. Nero caused Christians to be falsely accused and then to be condemned to the claws of wild beasts in the arena. When such cruelty is practiced against the innocent and helpless, we condemn the act. When Columbus was thrown into chains instead of being rewarded, we condemn the Spaniards. In the same way the real world of persons about us, the acts of parents, companions, and teachers are powerful in giving a good or bad tone to our sentiments, because, as living object lessons, their impress is directly and constantly upon us.

In such cases taken from daily experience and from illustrations of personal conduct in books, it is possible to observe *how moral judgments originate* and by repetition grow into convictions. They spring up naturally and surely when we understand well the circumstances under which an act was performed. The interest and sympathy felt for the persons lends great vividness to the judgments expressed. Each individual act stands out clearly and calls forth a prompt and unerring approval or disapproval. (But later the judgment must react upon our own conduct.) The examples are simple and objective, free from selfish interest on the child's part, so that good and bad acts are recognized in their true quality. These simple moral judgments are only a beginning, only a sowing of the seed. But harvests will not grow and ripen unless seed has been laid in the ground. It is a long road to travel before these early moral impressions develop into firm convictions which rule the conduct of an adult. But education is necessarily a slow process, and it is likely to be a perverted one unless the foundation is carefully laid in early years. The fitting way then to cultivate moral judgments, that is, to start just ideas of right and wrong, of virtues and vices, is by a regular and systematic presentation of persons illustrating noble and ignoble acts. A preference for the right and an aversion for the wrong will be the sure result of careful teaching. Habits of judging will be formed and strong moral convictions established which may be gradually brought to influence and control action.

A good share of the influences that are thrown around an ordinary child need to be counteracted. It can be done to a considerable extent *by instruction*. Many of the interesting characters of history are better company for us and for children than our neighbors and contemporaries. For the purposes of moral example and inspiration we may select as companions for them the best persons in history, provided we know how to select for ourselves and others. Their acts are personal, biographical, and interesting, and appeal at once to children as well as to their elders. There is no good reason why a much greater number of our school children should not be brought under the influence of the best books suited to their age. Here is a source of educational influence of high quality which is left too much to accident and to the natural, unaided instinct of children. A few get the benefit but many more are capable of receiving it. How much better the school choice and treatment of such books may be than the loose and miscellaneous reading of children, is discussed in Special Method. A fit introduction of children to this class of literature should be in the hands of teachers, and all the later reading of pupils will feel the salutary effect.

If this is the proper origin and culture of moral ideas, we desire to know how to utilize it in the common school course. It can only be done by an extensive use of historical and literary materials in all grades with the *conscious purpose* of shaping moral ideas and character. That the school has such influence at its disposal can not be reasonably denied by any one who believes that the family or the church can affect the moral character of their children. It may be objected that the school thus takes up the proper work of the home, when it ought to be occupied with other things. Would that the homes were all good! But even if they were the teacher could not fold his arms over a responsibility removed. As soon as a boy enters school, if not sooner, he begins, in some sense, to outgrow the home. New influences and interests find a lodgment in his affections. Companions, the wider range of his acquaintances, studies, and ambitions, share now with the home. John Locke objected radically to English public schools on this account. But even if we desired, we could not resort to private tutors as Locke did. The child is growing and changing. Who shall organize unity out of this maze of thoughts, interests, and influences, casting out the useless and bad, combining and strengthening the good? The more service the home renders the better. The child's range of thought and ambition is expanding. Who has the best survey of the field? In many cases at least, the teacher, especially where parents lack the culture and the children need a guide. Who spends six hours a day directing these currents of thought and interest? We are not disposed to underestimate the magnitude of the task here laid upon the teacher. The rights and duties of the home are not put in question. Indeed the spirit of this kind of teaching is best illustrated in a good home. A teacher who has a father's anxiety in the real welfare of children will not forget his duty in watching their moral growth. The moral atmosphere of a good home will remain the ideal for the school. In fact, Herbart's plan of education originated not in a school-room, but in an excellent home in Switzerland, where he spent three years in the private instruction of three boys. The conscientious zeal with which he devoted himself to the moral and mental growth of these children is a model for teachers. The shaping of three characters was, according to his view, entrusted to him. The common notion of intellectual growth and strength which rules in such cases was at once subordinated to *character development* in the moral sense. Not that the two ideas are at all antagonistic, but one is more important than the other. The selection of reading matter, of studies, and of employments, was adapted to each boy with a view to influencing conduct and moral action.

The Herbart school adheres to this view of education, and has *transferred its spirit and method to the schools*. The Herbartians have the hardihood, in this age of moral skeptics, to believe not only in moral example but also in moral teaching. (By moral skeptics we mean those who believe in morals but not in moral instruction.) They seek first of all historical materials of the richest moral content, in vivid personification, upon which to nourish the moral spirit of children. If properly treated, this subject matter will soon win the children by its power over feeling and judgment. With Crusoe the child goes through every hardship and success; with

Abraham he lives in tents, seeks pastures for his flocks, and generously marches out to the rescue of his kinsmen. He should not read Cæsar with a slow and toilsome drag (parsing and construing) that would render a bright boy stupid. If he goes with Cæsar at all, he must build an *agger*, fight battles, construct bridges, and approve or condemn Cæsar's acts. But we doubt the moral value of Cæsar's Gallic wars. By reading Plutarch we may see that the Latins and Greeks, before the days of their degeneracy, nourished their rising youth upon the traditions of their ancestry. The education produced a tough and sinewy brood of moral qualities. Their great men were great characters, largely because of the mother-milk of national tradition and family training. In Scotch, English, and German history we are familiar with Alfred, Bruce, Siegfried, and many other heroes of similar value in the training of youth.

It will be well for us to look into our own history and see what sort of a moral heritage of educative materials it has left us. What noble examples does it furnish of right thought and action? Have we any home-bred food like this for the nourishment of our growing youth? Our native American history is indeed nobler in tone and more abundant. For moral educative purposes in the training of the young the history of America, from the early explorations and settlements along the Atlantic coast to the present, has scarcely a parallel in history. It was a race of moral heroes that led the first colonies to many of the early settlements. Winthrop, Penn, Williams, Oglethorpe, Raleigh, and Columbus were great and simple characters, deeply moral and practical. For culture purposes, where can their equals be found? And where was given a better opportunity for the display of personal virtues than by the leaders of these little danger-encircled communities? The leaven of purity, piety, and manly independence which they brought with them and illustrated, has never ceased to work powerfully among our people. Why not bring the children into direct contact with these characters in the intermediate grades, not by short and sketchy stories, but by full life pictures of these men and their surroundings? We have not been wholly lacking in literary artists who have worked up a part of these materials into a more durable and acceptable form for our schools. We need to make an abundant use of this and other history for our boys and girls, not by devoting a year in the upper grades to a barren outline of American annals, but by a proper distribution of these and other similar rich treasures throughout the grades of the common school.

Tradition and fiction are scarcely less valuable than biography and history because of their vivid portrayal of strong and typical characters. Our own literature, and the world's literature at large, are a store-house well-stocked with moral educative materials, properly suited to children at different ages, if only sorted, selected, and arranged. But this requires broad knowledge of our best literature and clear insight into child character at different ages. This problem will not be solved in a day, nor in a life-time.

In making a progressive series of our best historical and literary products, it is necessary to select those materials which are better adapted than anything else to interest, influence, and mould the character of children at each time of life. It is now generally agreed by the best teachers that these selections shall be classical masterpieces, not in fragments but as wholes. They should be those classical materials that bear the stamp of genuine nobility. Goethe says "*The best is good enough for children.*" For some years past in our grammar grades we have been using some of the best selections of Whittier, Longfellow, Bryant, and others, and we are not even frightened by the length of such productions as Evangeline, The Lady of the Lake, or Julius Cæsar. A simple, adapted version of Robinson Crusoe is used in some schools as a second reader. From time immemorial choice selections of prose and verse have formed the staple of our readers above the third. But generally these selections are scrappy or fragmentary. Few of the great masterpieces have been used because most of them are supposed to be too long. Broken fragments of our choice literary products have been served up, but the best literary works as wholes have never been given to the children in the schools. The Greek youth were better served with the Iliad and Odyssey, and some of our grandfathers with the tales of the Old Testament. We now go still further back in the child-life and make use of fairy tales in the first grade. But many are not yet able to realize that select fairy stories are genuinely classical, that they are as well adapted to stimulate the minds of children as Hamlet the minds of adults. (See Special Method.)

The chief aim of our schools all along has not been an appreciation of literary masterpieces either in their moral or art value, but to acquire skill in reading, fluency, and naturalness, of expression. Our schools have been almost completely absorbed in the purely *formal* use of our literary materials, learning to read in the earlier grades and learning to read with rhetorical expression and confidence in the later ones. In the present argument our chief concern is not with the formal use of literary materials for practice in reading, but with the moral culture, conviction, and habit of life they may foster. Nor have we chiefly in view the *art* side of our best literary pieces. Appreciation of beauty in poetry and of strength in prose, admirable as they may be, are quite secondary to the main purpose. Coming in direct and vivid contact with manly deeds or with unselfish acts as personified in choice biography, history, fiction, and real life, will inspire children with thoughts that make life worth living. Neither formal skill in reading nor appreciation of literary art can atone for the lack of *direct moral incentive* which historical studies should give. All three ends should be reached.

Many teachers are now calling for a change in the spirit with which the best biography and literature are used. They call for an improvement in the quality and an increase in the quantity of complete historical episodes and of literary masterpieces. An appreciative reading of Ivanhoe revives the spirit of that age. The life of Samuel Adams is an epic that gives the youth a chance to live amid the stirring scenes of Boston in a notable time. Children are to live in thought and interest the lives of many men of other generations, as of Tell, Columbus, Livingstone, Lincoln, Penn, Franklin, Fulton. They are to partake of the experiences of the best typical men in the story of our own and of other countries.

The use of the best historical and literary works as a means of strengthening moral motives and principles with children whose minds and characters are developing, is a high aim in itself. And it will add *interest and life* to the formal studies, such as reading, spelling, grammar, and composition, which spring out of this valuable subject-matter.

History, in the broad sense, should be the chief constituent of a child's education. That subject-matter which contains the essence of moral culture in generative form deserves to constitute the chief mental food of young people. The conviction of the high moral value of historic subjects and of their peculiar adaptability to children at different ages, brings us to a positive judgment as to their relative value among studies. The first question, preliminary to all others in the common school course, "What is the most important study?" is answered by putting *history* at the head of the list.

Natural science takes the second place. In many respects it is co-ordinate with history. The object-world, which is so interesting, so informing, and so intimately interwoven with the needs, labors, and progress of men, furnishes the second great constituent of education for all children. Botany, zoology, and the other natural sciences, taken as a unit, constitute the field of nature apart from man. They furnish us an understanding of the varied objects and complex phenomena of nature. It is one of the imperative needs of all human minds that have retained their childlike thoughtfulness and spirit of inquiry, to desire to understand nature, to classify the variety of objects and appearances, to trace the chain of causes, and to search out the simple laws of nature's operations. The command early came to men to subdue the earth, and we understand better than primitive man that it is subdued through investigation and study. All the forces and bounties of nature are to be made serviceable to us and it can only be done by understanding her facts and laws. The road to mastery leads through patient observation, experiment, and study.

But we are concerned with the *educational* value of the natural sciences. Waitz says: "A correct philosophy of the world and of life is possible to a person only on the basis of a knowledge of one's self and of one's relation to surrounding nature." Diesterweg says: "No one can afford to neglect a knowledge of nature who desires to get a comprehension of the world and of God according to human possibility, or who desires to find his proper relation to Him and to real things. He who knows nothing of human history is an ignoramus, likewise he who knows nothing of natural science. To know nothing of either is a pure shame. Ignorance of nature is an unpardonable perversion." Kraepelin speaks as follows; "Instruction should open up to a pupil an understanding of the present, and thereby furnish a basis for a frank and many-sided philosophy of life, resting upon reality. But to the present belongs the world outside of us. Of this present there can be no such thing as an understanding unless it relates not only to inter-human relations but also to relations of man to animal, of animal to plant, and of organic life to inorganic life. The necessity of assuming a relation to our environment is unavoidable and this can only be done by acquainting ourselves with the surrounding world in every direction. This requirement would remain in force though man, like a god, were set above nature and her laws. But man lives, acts, and dies not outside of, but within the circle of nature's laws. This maxim is axiomatic and contains the final judgment against those who claim that a comprehensive but unified philosophy of life is possible without a knowledge of nature." Herbart says: "Here (in nature) lies the abode of real truth, which does not retreat before tests into an inaccessible past (as does history). This genuinely empirical character distinguishes the natural sciences and makes their loss irretrievable. It is here (in nature) that the object disentangles itself from all fancies and opinions and constantly stimulates the spirit of observation. Here then is found an obstruction to extravagant thinking such as the sciences themselves could not better devise." Ziller says: "The natural sciences are necessary in education because from the province of nature (as well as from history) are derived those means and resources which are necessary to accomplish the purposes of the will in action. Means and forces are the natural conditions for the realization of aims. Without knowledge of and intelligent power over nature, it is difficult to realize that certain aims are possible; action cannot be successful; will effort, based upon the firm conviction of ability, that is, judicious exercise of will, is impossible." We quote also from Professor Rein: "Let us observe in passing that in the great industrial contest between civilized nations, that people will suffer defeat which falls behind in the culture of natural science, and for this reason the motive of self-protection would demand natural science instruction. In favor of this teaching, the claim is further made that no science is so well adapted to train the mind to inductive thought processes as that which rests entirely upon induction, and that natural science study is in a position to resist more easily and successfully than all other studies, the deeply-rooted tendency in all branches to substitute words for ideas."

Rein (das vierte Schuljahr) explains further the leading ideas and standpoints which have appeared in historical order among science teachers in the common school. From the first crude ideas there has been marked progress toward higher aims in science teaching.

1. Natural history stories for *entertainment*. Many curious and entertaining facts in connection with animal life were searched out, more especially unusual and spicy anecdotes of shrewdness and intelligence. Some of the old readers, and even of the recent ones, are enriched with such marvels.

2. *Utility*, or the study of things in nature that are directly useful or hurtful to man. Whatever fruits or animals or herbs are of plain service to man, as well as things poisonous or dangerous, were studied because such information would be of future service. It was a purely practical aim, at first very narrow, but in an enlarged and liberal sense of much importance.

3. *Training of the senses* and of *the observing power*. By a study and description of natural objects, sense perception was to be sharpened and a habit of close observation formed. Among science teachers today no aim is more emphasized than this. It also stores away a body of useful ideas of great future value. This is an intellectual aim that accords better with the purpose of the school than the preceding.

4. *Analysis* and *determination of specimens*. To examine and trace a plant, mineral, or insect, to its true classification and name, has occupied much of the time of students. It requires nice discrimination, a comprehensive grasp of relations, and a power to seize and hold common characteristics. Many of our text-books and courses of study are based chiefly upon this idea.

5. *System-making*, or the reduction of all things in nature to a systematic whole, with a place for everything. Some of the greatest scientists, Linnaeus, for example, looked upon scientific classification as the chief aim of nature study. It has had a great influence upon schools and teachers. The attempt to compress everything into a system has led to many text-books which are but brief summaries of sciences like zoology, botany, and physics. Scientific classification is very important, but the attempt to make it a leading aim in teaching children is a mistake.

We may add that nature study is felt by all to offer abundant scope to the exercise of the esthetic faculty. There is great variety of beauty and gracefulness in natural forms in plant and animal; the rich or delicate coloring of the clouds, of birds, of insects, and of plants, gives constant pleasure. Then there are grand and impressive scenery and phenomena in nature, and melody and harmony in nature's voices.

These various aims of science study are valuable to the teacher as showing him the scope of his work. But a higher and more comprehensive standpoint has been reached. We now realize that the great purpose of this study is *insight into nature*, into this whole physical environment, with a view to a better appreciation of her objects, forces, and laws, and of their bearing on human life and progress.

All these purposes thus far developed in schools are to be considered as valuable subsidiary aims, leading up to the central purpose of the study of natural sciences, which is, "An understanding of life and of the powers and of the unity which express themselves in nature;" or, as Kraepelin says: "Nature should not appear to man as an inextricable chaos, but as a well-ordered mechanism, the parts fitting exactly to each other, controlled by unchanging laws, and in perpetual action and production." Humboldt is further quoted: "Nature to the mature mind is unity in variety, unity of the manifold in form and combination, the content or sum total of natural things and natural forces as a living whole. The weightiest result, therefore, of deep physical study is, by beginning with the individual, to grasp all that the discoveries of recent times reveal to us, to separate single things critically and yet not be overcome by the mass of details, mindful of the high destiny of man, to comprehend the mind of nature, which lies concealed under the mantle of phenomena." This sounds visionary and impracticable for children of the common school, especially when we know that much lower aims have not been successfully reached. In fact it cannot be said that the natural sciences have any recognized standing in the common school course. But it is worth the while to inquire whether natural sciences will ever be taught as they should be until the best attainable aims become the dominant principles for guiding teachers. Stripped of its rhetoric, the above mentioned aim, "an understanding of life and of the unity in nature," may prove a practical and inspiring guide to the teacher.

If we look upon nature as a field of observation and study which can be grasped as a whole both as a work of creation and as contributing in multiplied ways to man's needs, its proper study gives a many-sided culture to the mind. This leading purpose will bring into relation and unity all the subordinate aims of science teaching, such as information, utility, training of the senses and judgment, and of the power to compare and classify.

For the accomplishment of this great purpose of gaining *insight* into nature's many-sided activities, there are several simple means not yet mentioned. Running through nature are great principles and laws which can be studied upon concrete examples, plain and interesting to a child. The study of the squirrel in its home, habits, organs, and natural activities in the woods, will show how strangely adapted it is to its surroundings. But an observation of birds in the air and of fishes in water reveals the same curious fitness to surrounding nature. The study of plants and animals in their adaptation to environment, of the relation between organ and function; between organs, mode of life, and environment, leads up to a general law which applies to all plants and animals. The law of growth and development from the simple germ to the mature life form can be seen in the butterfly, the frog, and the sunflower. These laws and others in biology, if developed on concrete specimens, give much insight into the whole realm of nature, more stimulating by far than that based on scientific classifications, as orders, families and species. The great and simple outlines of nature's work begin to appear out of such laws.

Again the study of the whole *life history* of a plant or animal, in its relations to the inorganic world and to other plants and animals, is always a cross-section in the sciences and shows how all the natural sciences are knit together into a causal unity. Take the life history of a *hickory tree*. As it germinates and grows from the seed how it draws from the earth and air; the effect of storms, seasons, and lightning upon it; how it later furnishes nuts to the squirrels and boys; its branches may be the nesting place for birds and its bark for insects. Finally, the uses of its tough wood for man are seen. The life of a squirrel or of a honey-bee furnishes also a cross-section through all the sciences from the inorganic world up to man.

If in tracing life histories we take care to select *typical* subjects which exemplify perhaps thousands of similar cases, we shall materially shorten the road leading toward insight into nature. These types are concrete and have all the interest and attractiveness of individual life, but they also bring out characteristics which explain myriads of similar phenomena. A careful and detailed study of a single tree like the maple, with the circulation of the sap and the function of roots, bark, leaves, and woody fiber, will give an insight into the processes of growth upon which the life of the tree depends and these processes will easily appear to be true of all tree and plant forms.

In nature as it shows itself in the woods or in the pond, there is such a *mingling and interdependence* of the natural sciences upon each other that the book of nature seems totally different from books of botany, physics, and zoology as made by men. In the forest we find close together trees of many kinds, shrubs, flowering plants, vines, mosses, and ferns; grasses, beetles, worms, and birds; squirrels, owls and sunshine; rocks, soil, and springs; summer and winter; storms, frost, and drouth. Plants depend upon the soil and upon each other. The birds and squirrels find their home and food among the trees and plants. The trees seem to grow together as if they needed each other's companionship. All the plants and animals depend upon the soil, air, and climate, and the whole wood changes its garb and partly its guests with the seasons. A forest is a *life society*, consisting of mutually dependent parts. How nature disregards our conventional distinctions between the natural sciences! We need no better proof than this that they should not be taught chiefly from books. A child might learn a myriad of things in the woods and gain much insight into nature's ways without making any clear distinction between botany, zoology, and geology. Herein is also the proof that text-books are needed as a guide in nature's labyrinth. If the frequency and intimacy of mutual relations are any proof of unity, the natural sciences are a unit and have a right to be called by one name, *nature study*.

In the study of laws, life histories, and life groups, the *causal relations* in nature are found to be wonderfully stimulating to those who have begun to trace them out. The child as well as the mature scientist finds in these causal connections materials of absorbing interest.

It is plain, therefore, that the lines tending toward unity in nature study are numerous and strong; such as the scientific classifications of our text-books, the working out of general laws whether in biology or physics, the study of life histories in vegetable and animal, and the observation of life societies in the close mutual relations of the different parts or individuals.

If a course of nature studies is begun in the first grade and carried systematically through all the years up to the eighth grade, is it not reasonable to suppose that real insight into nature, based on observation taken at first hand, may be reached? It will involve a study of living plants and animals, minerals, physical apparatus and devices, chemical experiments, the making of collections, regular excursions for the observation of the neighboring fields, forests, and streams, and the working over of these and other concrete experiences from all sources through skillful class teaching.

The first great result to a child of such a series of studies is an intelligent and rational understanding of his home, the world, his natural environment. He will have a seeing eye and an appreciative mind for the thousand things surrounding his daily life where the ignorant toiler sees and understands nothing.

A second advantage which we can only hint at, while incidental is almost equally important. We have been considering nature chiefly as a realm by itself, apart from man. But the utilities of natural science in individual life and in society are so manifold that we accept many of the finest products of skill and art as if they were natural products—as if gold coins, silk dresses, and fine pictures grew on the bushes and only waited to be picked. The thousand-fold applications of natural science to human industry and comfort deserve to be perceived as *the result of labor and inventive skill*. Our much-lauded steam engines, telegraph microscopes, sewing machines, reapers, iron ships, and printing presses, are not examples of a few, but of myriads of things that natural science has secured. But how many children on leaving the common school understand the principle involved in any one of the machines mentioned, subjects of common talk as they are? As children leave the schools at fourteen or fifteen they should know and appreciate many such things, wherein man, by his wit and ingenious use of natures forces, has triumphed over difficulties. How are glass and soap made? What has a knowledge of natural science to do with the construction of stoves, furnaces, and lamps? How are iron, silver, and copper ore mined and reduced? How is sugar obtained from maple trees, cane, and beet root? How does a suction pump work and why? Without a knowledge of such applications of natural science we should be thrown back into barbarism. These things also, since they form such an important part of every child's environment, should be understood, but not for direct utility.

Historically considered, the study of natural science is the study of man's long continued struggle with nature and of his gradual triumph. It ends with insight into nature and into those contrivances of men by which her laws and forces are utilized. The whole subject of nature, her laws and powers, must not remain a sealed book to the masses of the people. Scientists, inventors, and scholars may lead the way, but they are only pioneers. The thousands of the children of the people are treading at their heels and must be initiated into the mysteries.

Our knowledge of these principles and appliances constitute in fact a good share of the foundation upon which our whole *culture status* rests. Without natural science we should understand neither nature nor society. Spencer shows the wide-reaching value of science knowledge in our modern life: "For leaving out only some very small classes, what are all men employed in? They are employed in the production, preparation, and distribution of commodities. And on what does efficiency in the production, preparation, and distribution of commodities depend? It depends on the use of methods fitted to the respective nature of these commodities, it depends on an adequate knowledge of their physical, chemical, or vital properties, as the case may be; that is, it depends on science. This order of knowledge which is in great part ignored in our school courses, is the order of knowledge underlying the right performance of all those processes by which civilized life is made possible. Undeniable as is this truth, and thrust upon us as it is at every turn, there seems to be no living consciousness of it. Its very familiarity makes it unregarded. To give due weight to our argument, we must therefore realize this truth to the reader by a rapid review of the facts." He then illustrates, in interesting detail, the varied applications of mathematics, physics, chemistry, biology, and social science to the industries and economies of real life, and concludes as follows: "That which our school courses leave almost entirely out, we thus find to be that which most nearly concerns the business of life. All our industries would cease were it not for that information which men begin to acquire as they best may after their education is said to be finished. And were it not for this information that has been from age to age accumulated and spread by unofficial means, these industries would never have existed. Had there been no teaching but such as is given, in our public schools, England would now be what it was in feudal times. That increasing acquaintance with the laws of nature which has through successive ages enabled us to subjugate nature to our needs, and in these days gives to the common laborer comforts which a few centuries ago kings could not purchase, is scarcely in any degree owed to the appointed means of instructing our youth. The vital knowledge—that by which we have grown as a nation to what we are, and which now underlies our whole existence—is a knowledge that has got itself taught in nooks and corners, while the ordained agencies for teaching have been mumbling little else but dead formulas." Spencer, *Education*, pp. 44, 54.

Not only the specialists in natural science, whose interest and enthusiasm are largely absorbed in these studies, but many other energetic teachers are persuaded that the culture value of nature studies is on a par with that of historical studies. But on account of the present lack of system and of clear purpose in natural science teachers, the first great problem in this field of common school effort is to select the material and perfect the method of studying nature with children.

Our estimate of the value of natural science for culture and for discipline is confirmed by the opinion of educational *reformers* and by the changes and progress in schools. An inquiry into the history of education in Europe and in America since the Reformation will show that the movement towards nature study has been accumulating momentum for more than three hundred years. In spite of the failure of such men as Comenius, Ratich, Basedow, and Rousseau to secure the introduction of these studies in a liberal degree, in spite of the enormous influence of custom and prejudice in favor of Latin and other traditional studies, the natural sciences have made recently such surprising advances and have so penetrated and transformed our modern life that we are simply compelled, even in the common school, to take heed of these great, living educational forces already at work.

The *universities* of England and of the United States have been largely transformed within the last forty years by the introduction, on a grand scale, of modern studies, particularly of the natural sciences. The fitting schools, academies, and high schools have had no choice but to follow this lead. Since the forces that produced this result in higher education sprang up largely outside of our institutions of learning, the movement is not likely to cease till the common school has been changed in the same way. The educational question of the future is not whether historical or natural science or formal studies are to monopolize the school course, but rather how these three indispensable elements of every child's education may be best harmonized and wrought into a unit.

But the question that confronts us at every turn is, *What is the disciplinary value of nature study*? We know, say the opponents, what a vigorous training in ancient languages and mathematics can do for a student. What results in this direction can the natural sciences tabulate? The champions of natural science point with pride to the great men who have been trained and developed in such studies. For inductive thinking the natural sciences offer the best materials. To cultivate self-reliance there is nothing like turning a student loose in nature under a skilled instructor. The spirit of investigation and of accurate thinking is claimed as a peculiar product of nature study. It is called, *par excellence*, "the scientific spirit." The undue reverence for authority produced by literary studies is not a weakness of natural science pursuits. But intense interest and devotion are combined with scientific accuracy and fidelity to nature and her laws.

We do not feel called upon to attempt a settlement of this dispute. We have already assumed that *history* in the broad sense (including languages) and *natural science* (or nature study) are the two great staples of the common school course, and that so far as discipline is concerned one is as important as the other. But we believe that those educators whose first, middle, and last question in education is, "What is the *disciplinary* value of a study?" have mistaken the primary problem of education. Just as in the proper training of the body, the strength and skill of a professional athlete are, in no sense, the true aim, but physical soundness, health, and vigor; so in mind culture, not extraordinary skill in mental gymnastics of the severest sort, is the essential aim, but mental soundness, integrity, and motive. The under-lying question in education is not, How strong or incisive is his mind? (This depends largely upon heredity and native endowment) but, What is its quality and its temper? If might is right, then mental strength is to be gained at all hazards. But if right is higher than might, then mental skill and power are only secondary aims. So long as we are dealing with fundamental aims in such a serious business as education, why stop short of that ideal which is manifestly the best? We have no controversy with the highest mental discipline and strength that are consistent with all-round mental soundness. Our better teachers are not lacking in appreciation for the value of what is called *formal mental discipline*, but they do generally lack faith in the innate power of the best studies to arouse interest and mental life. They emphasize the *drill* more than the *content* and the inspiration of the author. Both in theory and in practice they are greatly lacking in the intellectual sympathy and moral power which result from bringing the minds of students into direct contact with the noblest products of God's work in history and in the object world. Here we can put our finger on the radical weakness of our school work.

The really soul-inspiring teachers have not been formalists nor drill-masters alone. Friedrich August Wolf, for example, the great German philologist, was probably the most inspiring teacher of classical languages that Germany has had. But to what was his remarkable influence as a teacher of young men due? We usually think of a philologist as one who digs among the roots of dead languages, who worships the forms of speech and the laws of grammar. Doubtless he and his pupils were much taken up with these things, but they were not the prime source of his and their interest. Wolf defined philology as "the knowledge of human nature as exhibited in antiquity." He studied with great avidity everything that could throw light upon the lives, character, and language of the ancients. Their biographies, histories, geography, climate, dress, implements, their sculpture, monuments, buildings, tombs. Approaching the literature and language of the Greeks with this abundant knowledge of their real surroundings and conditions of life, he saw the deeper, fuller significance of every classical author and the great literary masterpieces were perceived as the expression of the national life. He appreciated language as the wonderful medium through which the more wonderful life of the versatile Greek expressed itself. The reason he was such a great philologist was because he was so great a realist, a man who was intensely interested in the Greek people, their history and life. Words alone had little charm for him. No great teacher has been simply a word-monger.

For the present we leave the question of discipline unanswered, though we are disposed to think that those studies which introduce children to the two great fields of real knowledge, and which arouse a strong desire to solve the problems found there, will also furnish the most valuable discipline.

The *formal studies* such as reading, spelling, writing, language, and much of arithmetic, have thus far appropriated the best share of school time. They are the tools for acquiring and formulating knowledge rather than knowledge itself. They are so indispensable in life that people have acquired a sort of superstitious respect for them. They are generally considered as of primary importance while other things are taken as secondary. By virtue of this excessive estimation the formal studies have become so strongly intrenched in the practice of the schools that they are really a heavy obstacle to educational progress. They have been so long regarded as the only gateway to knowledge that anyone who tries to climb in some other way is regarded as a thief and robber. We forget that Homer's great poems were composed and preserved for centuries before letters were invented. As more thought is expended on studies and methods of learning, the more the thinkers are inclined to exactly reverse the educational machinery. They say: "Thought studies must precede form studies." We should everywhere begin with valuable and interesting thought materials in history and natural science and let language, reading, spelling, and drawing follow. It is a thing much more easily said than done, but many active teachers are really doing it, and many others are wondering how it may be done. The advantage of putting the concrete realities of thought before children at first is that they give a powerful impetus to mental life, while pure formal studies in most cases have a deadening effect and gradually put a child to sleep. One of the great problems of school work is how to get more interest and instructive thought into school exercises.

We are now in a position to give a concluding estimate upon the relative value of these three elements in school education. History contributes the materials from which motives and moral impulses spring. It cultivates and strengthens moral convictions by the use of inspiring examples. The character of each child should be drawn into harmony with the highest impulses that men have felt. A desire to be the author of good to others should be developed into a practical ruling motive. Natural science on the other hand supplies a knowledge of the ordinary means and appliances by which the purposes of life are realized. It gives us proper insight into the conditions of life and puts us into intelligent relation to our environment. Not only must a child be supplied with the necessaries of life but he must appreciate the needs of health and understand the economies of society, such as the necessity of mental and manual labor, the right use of the products and forces of nature, and the advantage of men's inventions and devices. In a plan of popular education these two culture elements should mingle (history and natural science). In the case of all sorts of people in society the ability to execute high moral purposes depends largely upon a ready, practical insight into natural conditions. We are not thinking of the bread-and-butter phase of life and of the aid afforded by the sciences in making a living, but of the all-round, practical utility of natural science as a necessary supplement to moral training.

One of the best tests of a system of education is the preparation it gives for life in a liberal sense. When a child, leaving school behind, develops into a citizen, what tests are applied to him? The questions submitted to his judgment in his relations to the family and to society call for a quick and varied knowledge of men, insight into character, and for a large amount of practical information of natural science. He is asked to vote intelligently on social, political, sanitary, and economic questions; to judge of men's motives, opinions, and character; to vote upon or perhaps to direct the management of poor-houses, asylums, and penitentiaries; in towns to decide questions of drainage, police, water supply, public health, and school administration; to make contracts for public buildings, and bridges; to grant licenses and franchises; to serve on juries or as representatives of the people. These are not professional matters alone; they are the common duties of all citizens of a sound mind. These things each person should know how to judge, whether he be a blacksmith, a merchant, or a house keeper. In all such matters he must be not only a judge of others but an actor under the guidance of right motives and information. Again, in the bringing up of children, in the domestic arrangements of every home and in a proper care for the minds and bodies of both parents and children, a multitude of practical problems from each of the great fields of real knowledge must be met and solved.

A medical missionary illustrates this combination of historical and natural science elements. His life purpose is drawn from history, from the life of Christ, and from the traditional incentives of the church. The means by which he is to make himself practically felt are obtained from his study of medicine and from the sciences upon which it depends. These elements form the basis of his influence. This illustration however savors of professional rather than of general education, and we are concerned only with the latter. But the education of every child is analogous to that of the medical missionary in its two constituent elements.

As a matter of fact neither history nor natural science occupies any such prominence in the school course as we have judged fitting. Much thoughtful study, experience in teaching, and pioneer labor in partially new fields will be necessary in order to bring into existence such a course of study based upon the best materials. Many teachers already recognize the necessity for it and see before them a land of plenty as compared with the half-desert barrenness revealed in our present school course.

Two powerful convictions in the minds of those responsible for education have contributed to produce this desert-like condition in children's school employments, and this brings us to a discussion of the overestimation in which purely *formal studies* are held. The first article of faith rests upon the unshaken belief in the *practical studies,* reading, writing, and arithmetic. They are still looked upon as a barrier that must be scaled before the real work of education can begin. Learn to read, write, and figure and then the world of knowledge as well as of business is at your command. But many children find the barrier so difficult to scale that they really never get into the fields of knowledge. Many of our most thorough-going educators still firmly believe that a child can not learn anything worth mentioning till he has first learned to read. But however deeply rooted this confidence in the purely formal work of the early school years may be, it must break down as soon as means are devised for putting the realities of interesting knowledge before and underneath all the forms of expression. Let the necessity for expression spring from the real objects of study. Those children to whom the memorizing and drill upon forms of expression becomes tedious deserve our sympathy. There is a kind of knowledge adapted to arouse these dull ones to their full capacity of interest.

"Or what man is there of you whom if his son ask bread will he give him a stone?" With many a child the first reader, the arithmetic, or the grammar becomes a veritable stone. There is no good reason why the sole burden of work in early school grades should rest upon the learning of the pure formalities of knowledge. Children's minds are not adapted to an exclusive diet of this kind. The fact that children have good memories is no reason why their minds should be gorged with the dryest memory materials. They have a healthy interest in people, whether in life or in story, and in the objects in nature around them. What is thus pre-eminently true of the primary grades is true to a large extent throughout all the grades of the common school. It seems almost curious that the more tender the plants the more barren and inhospitable the soil upon which they are expected to grow. Fortunately these little ones have such an exuberance of life that it is not easily quenched. Formal knowledge stands first in our common school course and real studies are allowed to pick up such crumbs of comfort as may chance to fall. We believe in formal studies and in their complete mastery in the common school, but they should stand in the place of service to real studies. How powerful the tendency has been and still is toward pure formal drill and word memory is apparent from the fact that even geography and history, which are not at all formal studies, but full to overflowing with interesting facts and laws, have been reduced to a dry memorizing of words, phrases, and stereotyped sentences.

It is not difficult to understand why the numerous body of teachers, who easily drift into mechanical methods, has a preference for formal studies. They are comparatively easy and humdrum and keep pupils busy. Real studies, if taught with any sort of fitness, require energy, interest, and versatility, besides much outside work in preparing materials.

The second article of faith is a still stronger one. The better class of energetic teachers would never have been won over to formal studies on purely utilitarian grounds. A second conviction weighs heavily in their minds. "*The discipline of the mental faculties*" is a talisman of unusual potency with them. They prize arithmetic and grammar more for this than for any direct practical value. The idea of mental discipline, of training the faculties, is so ingrained into all our educational thinking that it crops out in a hundred ways and holds our courses of study in the beaten track of formal training with a steadiness that is astonishing. These friends believe that we are taking the back-bone out of education by making it interesting. The culmination of this educational doctrine is reached when it is said that the most valuable thing learned in school or out of it is to do and do vigorously that which is most disagreeable. The training of the will to meet difficulties unflinchingly is their aim, and we can not gainsay it. These stalwart apostles of educational hardship and difficulty are in constant fear lest we shall make studies interesting and attractive and thus undermine the energy of the will. But the question at once arises: Does not the will always act from *motives* of some sort? And is there any motive or incentive so stimulating to the will as a steady and constantly increasing *interest* in studies? It is able to surmount great difficulties.

We wish to assure our stalwart friends that we still adhere to the good old doctrine that "there is no royal road to learning." There is no way of putting aside the real difficulties that are found in every study, no way of grading up the valleys and tunneling through the hills so as to get the even monotony of a railroad track through the rough or mountainous part of education. Every child must meet and master the difficulties of learning for himself. There are no palace cars with reclining chairs to carry him to the summit of real difficulties. The *character-developing power* that lies in the mastery of hard tasks constitutes one of their chief merits. Accepting this as a fundamental truth in education, the problem for our solution is, how to stimulate children to encounter difficulties. Many children have little inclination to sacrifice their ease to the cause of learning, and our dull methods of teaching confirm them in their indifference to educational incentives. Any child, who, like Hugh Miller or Abraham Lincoln, already possesses an insatiable thirst for knowledge, will allow no difficulties or hardships to stand in the way of progress. This original appetite and thirst for knowledge which the select few have often manifested in childhood is more valuable than anything the schools can give. With the majority of children we can certainly do nothing better than to nurture such a taste for knowledge into vigorous life. It will not do to assume that the average of children have any such original energy or momentum to lead them to scale the heights of even ordinary knowledge. Nor will it do to rely too much upon a *forcing process*, that is, by means of threats, severity, and discipline, to carry children against their will toward the educational goal.

"Be not like dumb driven cattle,
Be a hero in the strife"

is sound educational doctrine.

The thing for teachers to do is to cultivate in children all healthy appetites for knowledge, to set up interesting aims and desires at every step, to lead the approach to different fields of knowledge in the spirit of conquest.

In the business world and in professional life men and women work with abundant energy and will because they have desirable ends in view. The hireling knows no such generous stimulus. Business life is full of irksome and difficult tasks but the aim in view carries people through them. We shall not eliminate the disagreeable and irksome from school tasks, but try to create in children such a spirit and ambition as will lead to greater exertions. To implant vigorous aims and incentives in children is the great privilege of the teacher. We shall some day learn that when a boy cracks a nut he does so because there may be a kernel in it, not because the shell is hard.

In concluding the discussion of relative values we will summarize the results.

History, in the liberal sense, surveys the field of human life in its typical forms and furnishes the best illustrative moral materials. *Nature study* opens the door to the real world in all its beauty, variety, and law. The *formal studies* constitute an indispensable part of useful and disciplinary knowledge, but they should occupy a secondary place in courses of study because they deal with the *form* rather than with the *content* of the sciences. It is a fundamental error to place formal studies in the center of the school course and to subordinate everything to their mastery. History and natural science, on the contrary, having the richest knowledge content, constitute a natural center for all educative efforts. They make possible a strong development of will-energy because their interesting materials furnish strong and legitimate incentives to mental activity and an enlarged field and opportunity to voluntary effort in pursuit of clear and attractive aims.

CHAPTER III.

NATURE OF INTEREST.

By interest we mean the natural bent or inclination of the mind to find satisfaction in a subject when it is properly presented. It is the natural attractiveness of the subject that draws and holds the attention. Interest belongs to the feelings but differs from the other feelings, such as desire or longing for an object, since it is satisfied with the simple contemplation without asking for possession. The degree of interest with which different kinds of knowledge are received, varies greatly. Indeed, it is possible to acquire knowledge in such a manner as to produce dislike and disgust. A proper interest in a subject leads to a quiet, steady absorption of the mind with it, but does not imply an impetuous, passionate, and one-sided devotion to one thing. Interest keeps the mind active and alert without undue excitement or partiality.

It would be well if every study and every lesson could be sustained by such an interest as this. It would be in many cases like lubricating oil poured upon dry and creaking axles. Knowledge might then have a flavor to it and would be more than a consumption of certain facts and formulas coldly turned over to the memory machine. The child's own personality must become entangled in the facts and ideas acquired. There should be a sort of affinity established between the child's soul and the information he gains. At every step the sympathy and life experiences from without the school should be intertwined with school acquisitions. All would be woven together and permeated by *feeling*. We forget that the feelings or sensibilities awakened by knowledge are what give it personal significance to us.

The interest we have in mind is *intrinsic,* native to the subject, and springs up naturally when the mind is brought face to face with something attractive. The things of sense in nature and the people whom we see and read about, have a perennial and inexhaustible attraction for us all. It is among these objects that poets and artists find their materials and their inspiration. For the same reason the pictures drawn by the artist or poet have a charm which does not pass away. They select something concrete and individual; they clothe it with beauty and attractiveness; they give it some inherent quality that appeals to our admiration and love. It must call forth some esthetic or moral judgment by virtue of its natural quality. Like luscious grapes the objects presented to the thought of the children should have an unquestionable quality that is desirable.

We just spoke of interest, not as fluctuating and variable, but steady and persistent. It contains also the elements of ease, pleasure, and needed employment;

that is, in learning something that has a proper interest, there is greater ease and pleasure in the acquisition, and occupation with the object satisfies an inner need. "When interest has been fully developed, it must always combine pleasure, facility, and the satisfaction of a need. We see again that in all exertions, power and pleasure are secured to interest. It does not feel the burden of difficulties but often seems to sport with them."—*Ziller*.

A natural interest is also awakened by what is strange, mysterious, and even frightful, but these kinds of interest concern us from a speculative rather than a pedagogical point of view. We are seeking for those interests which contribute to a normal and permanent mental action.

Severe effort and exertion are a necessary part of instruction, but a proper interest in the subject will lead children to exert themselves with greater energy even when encountering disagreeable tasks. There are places in every subject when work is felt as a burden rather than as a pleasure, but the interest and energy aroused in the more attractive parts will carry a child through the swamps and mires at a speedier rate. It is not at all desirable to conceal difficulties under the guise of amusement. But by means of a natural interest it is possible to bring the mind into the most favorable state for action. In opposition to a lively and humane treatment of subjects, a dry and dull routine has often been praised as the proper discipline of the mind and will. "It was a mistake," says Ziller, "to find in the simple pressure of difficulties a source of culture, for it is the opposite of culture. It was a mistake to call the pressure of effort, the feeling of burden and pain, a source of proper training, simply because will power and firmness of character are thus secured and preserved to youth. Pedagogical efforts looking towards a lightening and enlivening of instruction should not have been answered by an appeal to severe methods, to strict, dry, and dull learning, that made no attempt to adapt itself to the natural movement of the child's mind." (Ziller, Lehre vom E. U., p. 355.) Not those studies which are driest, dullest, and most disagreeable should be selected upon which to awaken the mental forces of a child, but those which naturally arouse his interest and prompt him to a lively exercise of his powers. For children of the third and fourth grade to narrate the story of the Golden Fleece is a more suitable exercise than to memorize the CXIXth Psalm, or a catechism.

A proper interest aims, finally, at the highest form of *quiet, sustained will exertion*. The succession of steps leading up to will energy, is interest, desire, and will. Before attempting to realize the higher forms of will effort, we must look to the fountains and sources out of which it springs. If a young man has laid up abundant and interesting stores of knowledge of architecture, he only needs an opportunity, and there is likely to be great will-energy in the work of planning and constructing buildings. But without this interest and knowledge there will be no effort along this line. In like manner children cannot be expected to show their best effort unless the subject is made strongly interesting from the start, or unless interest-awakening knowledge has already been stored in the mind. To make great demands upon the will power in early school years, is like asking for ripe fruits before they have had time to mature. Knowledge, feelings, and will-incentives of every sort must be first planted in the mind, before a proper will-energy can be expected. In teaching, we should aim to develop will power, not to take it for granted as a ready product. As the will should ultimately control all the mental powers, its proper maturity is a later outcome of education. Even supposing that the will has considerable original native power, it is a power that is likely to lie dormant or be used in some ill-direction, unless proper incentives are brought to bear upon it. The will is so constituted that it is open to appeal, and in all the affairs of school and life, incentives of all sorts are constantly brought to bear upon it. Why not make an effort to bring to bear the incentives that spring out of interest, that steady force, which is able to give abiding tendency and direction to the efforts? Why not cultivate those nobler incentives that spring out of culture-bringing-knowledge? There are, therefore, important preliminaries to full will energy, which are secured by the cultivation of knowledge, the sensibilities, and desires.

There is a common belief that any subject can be made interesting if only the teacher knows the secret of the how; if only he has proper *skill*. But it is hard even for a skillful workman "to make bricks without straw," to awaken mental effort where interest in the subject is entirely lacking. It is often claimed that if there is dullness and disgust with a study it is the fault of the teacher. As Mr. Quick says, "I would go so far as to lay it down as a rule, that whenever children are inattentive and apparently take no interest in a lesson, the teacher should always look first to himself for the reason. There are perhaps no circumstances in which a lack of interest does not originate in the mode of instruction adopted by the teacher." This statement assumes that all knowledge is about equally interesting to pupils, and everything depends upon the *manner* in which the teacher deals with it. But different kinds of knowledge differ widely in their power to awaken interest in children. The true idea of interest demands that the subject matter be *in itself* interesting, adapted to appeal to a child, and to secure his participation. If the interest awakened by bringing the mind in contact with the subject is not spontaneous, it is not genuine and helpful in the best sense. One of the first and greatest evils of all school courses has been a failure to select those subjects, which in themselves are adapted to excite the interest of children at each age of progress. If we could assume that lessons had been so arranged, we might then with Mr. Quick justly demand of a teacher a manner of teaching that must make the subjects interesting, or in other words a manner of treatment that would be appropriate to an interesting subject.

There are two kinds of interest that need to be clearly distinguished: *direct* interest, which is felt for the thing itself, for its own sake, and *indirect* interest which points to something else as the real source. A miser loves gold coins for their own sake, but most people love them only because of the things for which they may be exchanged. The poet loves the beauty and fragrance of flowers, the florist adds to this a mercenary interest. A snow-shovel may have no interest for us ordinarily, but just when it is needed, on a winter morning, it is an object of considerable interest. It is simply a means to an end. The kind of interest which we think is so valuable for instruction is direct and intrinsic. The life of Benjamin Franklin calls out a strong direct interest in the man and his fortunes. A humming bird attracts and appeals to us for its own sake. Indirect interest, so called, has more of the character of *desire*. A desire to restore one's health will produce great interest in a certain health resort, like the Hot Springs, or in some method of treatment, as the use of Koch's lymph. The desire for wealth and business success will lead a merchant in the fur trade to take interest in seals and seal-fishing, and in beavers, trapping, etc. The wish to gain a prize will cause a child to take deep interest in a lesson. But in all these cases desire *precedes* interest. Interest, indeed, in the thing itself for its own sake, is frequently not present. It is true in many cases that indirect interest is not interest at all. It is a dangerous thing in education to substitute *indirect* for *direct* or true interest. The former often means the cultivation, primarily, of certain inordinate desires or feelings, such as rivalry, pride, jealousy, ambition, reputation, love of self. By appealing to the selfish pride of children in getting lessons, hateful moral qualities are sometimes started into active growth in the very effort to secure the highest intellectual results and discipline. Giving a prize for superiority often produces jealousy, unkindness, and deep-seated ill-will where the cultivation of a proper natural interest would lead to more kindly and sympathetic relations between the children. The cultivation of direct interest in all valuable kinds of knowledge, on the other hand, leads also to the cultivation of desires, but the desires thus generated are pure and generous, the desire for further knowledge of botany or history, the desire to imitate what is admirable in human actions and to shun what is mean. The desires which spring out of direct interest are elevating, while the desires which are associated with indirect interest are in many cases egotistic and selfish.

We often say that it is necessary to make a subject interesting so that it may be more *palatable*, more easily learned. This is the commonly accepted idea. It is a means of helping us to swallow a distasteful medicine. If the main purpose were to get knowledge into the mind, and interest only a means to this end, the cultivation of such indirect interests would be all right. But interest is one of the qualities which we wish to see permanently associated with knowledge even after it is safely stored in the mind. If interest is there, future energy and activity will spring spontaneously out of the acquirements. Indirect interest indeed is often necessary and may be a sign of tact in teaching. But it is negative and weak in after results. So far as it produces motives at all they may be dangerous. It cannot build up and strengthen character but threatens to undermine it by cultivating wrong motives. There is no assurance that knowledge thus acquired can affect the will and bear fruit in action, even though it be the right kind of knowledge, because it is not the knowledge in this case that furnishes the incentives. The interest that is awakened in a subject because of its innate attractiveness, leaves incentives which may ripen sooner or later into action. The higher kind of interest is direct, intrinsic, not simply receptive, but active and progressive. In the knowledge acquired it finds only incentives to further acquisition. It is life giving and is prompted by the objects themselves, just as the interest of boys is awakened by deeds of adventure and daring or by a journey into the woods. The interest in an object that springs from some other source than the thing itself, is indirect, as the desire to master a lesson so as to excel others, or gain a prize, or make a money profit out of it. In speaking of interest in school studies, teachers quite commonly have only the indirect in mind; *i.e.*, the kind that leads children to take hold of and master their lessons more readily.

Interest is thus chiefly a means of overcoming distasteful tasks. It is the merit of a direct or genuine interest that it aids in mastering difficulties and in addition to this gives a permanent pleasure in studies. One of the high aims of instruction is to implant a strong permanent interest in studies that will last through school days and after they are over.

A live interest springs most easily out of *knowledge subjects* like history and natural science. Formal studies like grammar and arithmetic awaken it less easily. Herbart has classified the chief kinds and sources of interest as follows: Interest in nature apart from man, and interest in man, society, etc. In *nature* and natural objects as illustrated in the natural sciences there are three chief kinds of interest. *Empirical,* which is stirred by the variety and novelty of things seen. There is an attractiveness in the many faces and moods of nature. Between the years of childhood and old age there is scarcely a person who does not enjoy a walk or a ride in the open air, where the variety of plant, bird, animal, and landscape makes a pleasing panorama. *Speculative* interest goes deeper and inquires into the relations and causal connections of phenomena. It traces out similarities and sequences, and detects law and unity in nature. It is not satisfied with the simple play of variety, but seeks for the cause and genesis of things. Even a child is anxious to know how a squirrel climbs a tree or cracks a nut; where it stores its winter food, its nest and manner of life in winter. Why is it that a mole can burrow and live under ground? How is it possible for a fish to breathe in water? *Esthetic* interest is awakened by what is beautiful, grand, and harmonious in nature or art. The first glance at great overhanging masses of rock, oppresses us with a feeling of awe. The wings of an insect, with their delicate tracery and bright hues, are attractive, and stir us with pleasure. The graceful ferns beside the brooks and moss-stained rocks suggest fairy-land.

But stronger even than these interests which attach us to the things of nature, are the interests of *humanity.* The concern felt for others in joy or sorrow is based upon our interest in them individually, and is *sympathetic.* In this lies the charm of biography and the novel. Take away the personal interest we have in Ivanhoe, Quenten Durward, etc., and Scott's glory would quickly depart. What empty and spiritless annals would the life of Frederic the Great and Patrick Henry furnish! *Social* interest is the regard for the good or evil fortune of societies and nations. Upon this depends our concern for the progress of liberty and the struggle for free institutions in England and other countries. On a smaller scale clubs, fraternities, and local societies of all kinds are based on the social interest. *Religious* interest finally reveals our consciousness of man's littleness and weakness, and of God's providence. As Pestalozzi says, "God is the nearest resource of humanity." As individuals or nations pass away their fate lies in His hand.

The *sources* of interest therefore are varied and productive. Any one of the six is unlimited in extent and variety. Together they constitute a boundless field for a proper cultivation of the emotional as well as intellectual nature of man. A study of these sources of genuine interest and a partial view of their breadth and depth, reveals to teachers what our present school courses tend strongly to make them forget, namely, that the right kind of knowledge contains in itself the stimulus and the germs to great mental exertion. The dull drill upon grammar, arithmetic, reading, spelling, and writing, which are regarded as so important as to exclude almost everything else, has convinced many a child that school is veritably a dull place. And many a teacher is just as strongly convinced that keeping school is a dull and sleepy business. And yet the sources of interest are abundant to overflowing for him who has eyes to see. That these sources and materials of knowledge, arousing deep and lasting interests, are above other things adapted to children and to the school room, is a truth worthy of all emphasis.

Interest is a good test of the *adaptability* of knowledge. When any subject is brought to the attention at the right age and in the proper manner, it awakens in children a natural and lively feeling. It is evident that certain kinds of knowledge are not adapted to a boy at the age of ten. He cares nothing about political science, or medicine, or statesmanship, or the history of literature. These things may be profoundly interesting to a person two or three times as old, but not to him. Other things, however, the story of Ulysses, travel, animals, geography, and history, even arithmetic, may be very attractive to a boy of ten. It becomes a matter of importance to select those studies and parts of studies for children at their changing periods of growth, which are adapted to awaken and stimulate their minds. We shall be saved then from doing what the best of educators have so frequently condemned, namely, when the child asks for bread give him a stone, or when he asks for fish give him a serpent.

The neglect to take proper cognizance of this principle of *interest* in laying out courses of study and in the manner of presenting subjects is certainly one of the gravest charges that ever can be brought against the schools. It is a sure sign that teachers do not know what it means "to put yourself in his place," to sympathize with children and feel their needs. The educational reformers who have had deepest insight into child-life, have given us clear and profound warnings. Rousseau says: "Study children, for be sure you do not understand them. Let childhood ripen in children. The wisest apply themselves to what it is important to *men* to know, without considering what *children* are in a condition to learn. They are always seeking the man in the child, without reflecting what he is before he can be a man." It is well for us to take these words home and act upon them.

It is worth the trouble to inquire whether it is possible to select subjects for school study which will prove essentially attractive and interesting from the age of six on. *Are* there materials for school study which are adapted fully to interest first grade children? We know that fairy stories appeal directly to them, and they love to reproduce them. Reading and spelling in connection with these tales are also stirring studies. Reading a familiar story is certainly a much more interesting employment than working at the almost meaningless sentences of a chart or first reader. Number work when based upon objects can be made to hold the attention of little ones, at least in the last half of the first grade. They love also to see and describe flowers, rocks, plants, and pictures. It probably requires more skillful teaching to awaken and hold the interest in the first grade than in the second or any higher grade, unless older children have been dulled by bad instruction. On what principle is it possible to select both interesting and valuable materials for the successive grades? We will venture to answer this difficult question.

The main interest of children must be attracted by what we may call *real knowledge* subjects; that is, those treating of people (history stories, etc.,) and those treating of plants, animals, and other natural objects (natural science topics). Grammar, arithmetic, and spelling are chiefly form studies and have less native attraction for children. Secondly, it may be laid down as a fact of experience that children will be more touched and stimulated by *particular* persons and objects in nature than by any *general* propositions, or laws, or classifications. They prefer seeing a particular palm tree to hearing a general description of palms. A narrative of some special deed of kindness moves them more than a discourse on kindness. They feel a natural drawing toward real, definite persons and things, and an indifference or repulsion toward generalities. They prefer the story to the moral. Children are little materialists. They dwell in the sense-world, or in the world of imagination with very clear and definite pictures.

But while dealing with *things of sense* and with particulars, it is necessary in teaching children to keep an eye directed toward general classes and toward those laws and principles that will be fully appreciated later. In geography, arithmetic, language lessons, and natural science, we must collect more materials in the lower grades; more simple, concrete illustrations. They are the basis upon which we can soon begin to generalize and classify. The more attractive the illustrative materials we select, the stronger the appeal to the child's own liking, the more effective will be the instruction. A way has been discovered to make the study of the concrete and individual lead up with certainty to the grasp of general notions and even of scientific laws as fast as the children are ready for them. If the concrete object or individual is carefully selected it will be a *type*, that is, it illustrates a whole class of similar objects. Such a typical concrete object really combines the particular and the general. It has all the advantage of object-teaching, the powerful attraction of real things, but its comparison with other objects will also show that it illustrates a general law or principle of wide-reaching scientific importance. In both these steps natural interest is provided for in the best way. A full and itemized examination of some attractive object produces as strong an interest as a child is capable of. Then to find out that this object is a sort of key to the right interpretation of other objects, more or less familiar to him, has all the charm of discovery. The *sunflower*, for example, is a large and attractive object for itemized study. It the examination leads a step further to a comparison with other composite flowers, there will be an interesting discovery of kinship with dandelions, asters, thistles, etc. This principle of the type, as illustrating both the particular and general, is true also of geographical topics that lead a child far from home and call for the construction of mental pictures. The study of *Pike's Peak* and vicinity is very interesting and instructive for fourth grade children. The valleys, springs at Manitou, Garden of the Gods, Cheyenne Canon and Falls, the Cave of the Winds, the ascent of the peak by trail or by railroad, the views of distant mountains, the summit house on the barren and rugged top, the snow fields even in summer, the drifting mists that shut off the view, the stories of hardship and early history—these things take a firm hold on a child's interest and desire for knowledge. When this whole picture is reasonably complete a brief comparison of Pike's Peak with Mt. Washington, Mt. Marcy, Mt. Shasta, and Mt. Rainier, will bring forth points of contrast and similarity that will surprise and instruct a child. In every branch of study there are certain underlying principles and forms of thought whose thorough mastery in the lower grades is necessary to successful progress. They are the important and central ideas of the subject. It was a marked quality of Pestalozzi to sift out these simple fundamentals and to master them. It is for us to make these simple elements intelligible and interesting by the use of concrete *types* and illustrations drawn from nature and from human life. If we speak of history and nature as the two chief subjects of study, the simple, fundamental relations of persons to each other in society, and the simple, typical objects, forces, and laws of nature constitute the basis of all knowledge. These elements we desire to master. But to make them attractive to children, they should not be presented in bald and sterile outlines, but in typical forms. All actions and human relations must appear in attractive *personification*.

Persons speak and act and virtues shine forth in them. We do not study nature's laws at first, but the beautiful, *typical life forms* in nature, the lily, the oak, Cinderella, and William Tell. For children, then, the underlying ideas and principles of every study, in order to start the interest, must be revealed in the most beautiful illustrative forms which can be furnished by nature, poetry, and art. The story of William Tell, although it comes all the way from the Alps and from the distant traditional history of the Swiss, is one of the best things with which to illustrate and impress manliness and patriotism. The fairy stories for still younger children, are the best means for teaching kindness or unselfishness, because they are so chaste, and beautiful, and graceful, even to the child's thought. The most attractive type-forms and life-personifications of fundamental ideas in history and nature are the really interesting objects of study for children. To put it in a simple, practical form—objects and human actions, if well selected, are the best means in the world to excite curiosity and the strong spirit of inquiry. While dwelling upon this thought of the attractiveness of type-forms as personified in things or persons, we catch a glimpse of a far-reaching truth in education.

The idea of *culture epochs*, as typical of the steps of progress in the race, and also of the periods of growth in the child, offers a deep perspective into educational problems. In the progress of mankind from a primitive state of barbarism to the present state of culture in Europe and in the United States, there has been a succession of not very clearly defined stages. In point of government, for example, there has been the savage, nomad, patriarch, kingdom, constitutional monarchy, democracy, republic, federal republic. There have been great epochs of political convulsion in the conflicts with external powers and in civil struggles and revolutions. In the growth of handicrafts, arts, manufactures, and inventions, there has been a series of advances from the time when men first began to cultivate the ground, to reduce the metals, and to bring the forces of nature into service. In the development of human society, therefore, and in the progress of arts and human knowledge, there are certain typical stages whose proper use may help us to solve some of the difficult problems in educating the young. All nations have passed through some of these important epochs. The United States, for example, since the first settlements upon the east coast, have gone rapidly through many of the characteristic epochs of the world's history, in politics, commerce, and industry; in social life, education, and religion.

The importance of the culture epochs for schools lies in the theory, accepted by many great writers, that children in their growth from infancy to maturity, pass through a series of steps which correspond broadly to the historical epochs of mankind. A child's life up to the age of twenty, is a sort of epitome of the world's history. Our present state of culture is a result of growth, and if a child is to appreciate society as it now is, he must grow into it out of the past, by having traveled through the same stages it has traced. But this is only a very superficial way of viewing the relation between child and world history. The periods of child life are so similar to the epochs of history, that a child finds its *proper mental food* in the study of the materials furnished by these epochs. Let us test this. A child eight years old cares nothing about reciprocity or free silver, or university extension. Robinson Crusoe, however, who typifies mankind's early struggle with the forces of nature, claims his undivided attention. A boy of ten will take more delight in the story of King Alfred or William Tell than in twenty Gladstones or Bismarcks. Not that Gladstone's work is less important or interesting to the right person, but the boy does not live and have his being in the Gladstonian age. Not all parts of history, indeed, are adapted to please and instruct some period of youth. Whole ages have been destitute of such materials, barren as deserts for educational purposes. But those epochs which have been typical of great experiences, landmarks of progress, have also found poets and historians to describe them. The great works of poets and historians contain also the great *object lessons* upon which to cultivate the minds of children. Some of the leading characters of fiction and history are the best personifications of the steps of progress in the history of the race; Crusoe, Abraham, Ulysses, Alfred, Tell, David, Charlemagne, Moses, Columbus, Washington. These men, cast in a large and heroic mold, represent great human strivings and are adapted to teach the chief lessons of history, if properly selected and arranged. These typical individual characters illustrate the fundamental ideas that will give insight and appreciation for later social forms. They contain, hidden as it were, the essential part of great historical and social truths of far-reaching importance. The culture epochs will be seen later to be important in solving the problem of the *concentration of instruction* along certain lines, but in the present discussion their value is chiefly seen in their adaptability to arouse the interest of children, by supplying peculiarly congenial materials of instruction in the changing phases of child progress.

The interest most worth awakening in pupils is not only direct but *permanent*. Hawthorne's Golden Touch embodies a simple classic truth in such transparent form that its reperusal is always a pleasure. In the same way, to observe the autumn woods and flowers, the birds and insects, with sympathy and delight, leaves a lasting pleasure in the memory. The best kind of knowledge is that which lays a permanent hold upon the affections. The best method of learning is that which opens up any field of study with a growing interest. To awaken a child's permanent interest in any branch of knowledge is to accomplish much for his character and usefulness. An enduring interest in American history, for example, is valuable in the best sense, no matter what the method of instruction. Any companion or book that teaches us to observe the birds with growing interest and pleasure has done what a teacher could scarcely do better. This kind of knowledge becomes a living, generative culture influence. Knowledge which contains no springs of interest is like faith divorced from works. Information and discipline may be gained in education without any lasting interest, but the one who uses such knowledge and discipline is only a machine. A Cambridge student who had taken the best prizes and scholarships said at the end of his university career: "I am at a loss to know what to do. I have already gained the best distinctions, and I can see but little to work for in the future." The child of four years, who opens his eyes with unfeigned interest and surprised inquiry into the big world around him, has a better spirit than such a dead product of university training. But happily this is not the spirit of our universities now. The remarkable and characteristic idea in university life today is the spirit of investigation and scientific inquiry which it constantly awakens. We happen to live in a time when university teachers are trying to enlarge the bounds of human knowledge in every direction, to solve problems that have not been solved before. No matter what the subject, the real student soon becomes an explorer, an investigator in fields of absorbing interest. The common school can scarcely do better than to receive this generous impulse into its work. Can our common studies be approached in this inquisitive spirit? Can growth in knowledge be made a progressive investigation? A true interest takes pleasure in acquired knowledge, and standing upon this vantage looks with inquiring purpose into new worlds. Children in our schools are sometimes made so dyspeptic that no knowledge has any relish. But the soul should grow strong, and healthy, and elastic, upon the food it takes. If the teaching is such that the appetite becomes stronger, the mental digestion better, and if the spirit of interest and inquiry grows into a steady force, the best results may be expected.

The cultivation of a *many-sided interest* is desirable in order to *avoid* narrowness, and to open up the various sources of mental activity, *i.e.*, to stimulate mental vigor along many lines. We believe that most children are capable of taking interest in many kinds of study. The preference which some children show for certain branches and the dislike for others may be due to peculiar early surroundings, and is often the result of good or poor teaching as much as to natural gifts. As every child has sympathies for companions and people, so every child may take a real interest in story, biography, and history, if these subjects are rightly approached. So also the indifference to plant and animal life shown by many persons is due to lack of culture and suitable suggestion at the impressionable age. Unquestionably the lives of most people run in too narrow a channel. They fail to appreciate and enjoy many of the common things about them, to which their eyes have not been properly opened. The particular trade or business so engrosses most people's time that their sympathies are narrowed and their appreciation of the duties and responsibilities of life is stunted. The common school, more than all other institutions, should lay broad foundations and awaken many-sided sympathies. The trade school and the university can afford to specialize, to prepare for a vocation. The common school, on the contrary, is preparing all children for general citizenship. The narrowing idea of a trade or calling should be kept away from the public school, and as far as possible varied interests in knowledge should be awakened in every child.

But this variety of interests may lead to scattering and *superficial knowledge.* And in its results many-sided interest would seem to point naturally to many-sided activity; that is, to multiplicity of employments, to that character which in Yankee phrase is designated as "Jack of all trades and master of none." If instead of being allowed to spread out so much, the educational stream is confined between narrow banks, it will show a deep and full current. If allowed to spread over the marshes and plains, it becomes sluggish and brackish. Our course of study for the common schools in recent years, has been largely added to and has been extended over the whole field of knowledge. History, geography, natural science lessons and drawing have been added to the old reading, writing, arithmetic, and grammar. There may appear to be more variety, but less strength. When in addition to this greater variety of studies, enthusiastic teachers desire to increase the *quantity* of knowledge in each branch and to present as many interesting facts as possible, at every point, we have the *over-loading* of the school course. This effect will be noticed in a later chapter in its bearing upon concentration. Children have too much to learn. They become pack-horses, instead of free spirits walking in the fields of knowledge. *Mental vigor,* after all, is worth more than a mind grown corpulent and lazy with an excess of pabulum, overfed. The cultivation therefore of a many-sided interest ceases to be a blessing as soon as encyclopedic knowledge becomes its aim. In fact the desire on the part of teachers to make the knowledge of any subject complete and encyclopedic destroys all true interest. The solution of this great problem does not consist in identifying many-sided interest with encyclopedic knowledge, but in such a detailed study of *typical* forms in each case as will give insight into that branch without any pretension to exhaustive knowledge. Certainly a true interest in plants does not require that we become acquainted with all the species of all the genera. But a proper study of a few typical forms in a few of the families and genera might produce a much deeper interest in nature and in her laws.

The culture of a many-sided interest is essential to a full development and *perfection* of the mental activities. It is easy to see that interest in any subject gives all thought upon it a greater vigor and intensify. Mental action in all directions is strengthened and vivified by a direct interest. On the other hand mental life diminishes with the loss of interest, and even in fields of knowledge in which a man has displayed unusual mastery, a loss of interest is followed by a loss of energy. Excluding interest is like cutting off the circulation from a limb. Perfect vigor of thought which we aim at in education, is marked by strength along three lines, the vigor of the individual ideas, the extent and variety of ideas under control, and the connection and harmony of ideas. It is the highest general aim of intellectual education to strengthen mental vigor in these three directions. Many-sided interest is conducive to all three. Every thought that finds lodgment in the mind is toned up and strengthened by interest. It is also easier to retain and reproduce some idea that has once been grasped with full feeling of interest. An interest that has been developed along all leading lines of study has a proper breadth and comprehensiveness and cannot be hampered and clogged by narrow restraints and prejudice. We admire a person not simply because he has a few clear ideas, but also for the extent and variety of this sort of information. Our admiration ceases when he shows ignorance or prejudice or lack of sympathy with important branches of study. Finally, the unity and harmony of the varied kinds of knowledge are a great source of interest. The tracing of connections between different studies and the insight that comes from proper associations, are among the highest delights of learning. The connection and harmony of ideas will be discussed under concentration.

The six interests above mentioned are to be developed along parallel lines. They are to be kept in proper *equipoise*. It is not designed that anyone shall be developed to the overshadowing of the others. They are like six pillars upon which the structure of a liberal education is rested. A cultivation of any one, exclusively, may be in place when the work of general education is complete and a profession or life labor has been chosen.

It is also true that a proper interest is a *protection* against the desires, disorderly impulses, and passions. One of the chief ends of education is to bring the inclinations and importunate desires under mastery, to establish a counterpoise to them by the steady and persistent forces of education. A many-sided interest cultivated along the chief paths of knowledge, implies such mental vigor and such preoccupation with worthy subjects as naturally to discourage unworthy desires.

Locke says, self-restraint, the mastery over one's inclinations, is the foundation of virtue. "He that has found a way how to keep a child's spirit easy, active, and free, and yet at the same time to restrain him from many things he has a mind to, and to draw him to things that are uneasy to him; he, I say, that knows how to reconcile these seeming contradictions, has, in my opinion, got the true secret of education." But it is a secret still; the central question remains unanswered. How is the teacher to approach and influence the will of the child? Is it by supposing that the child has a will already developed and strong enough to be relied upon on all occasions? On the contrary, must not the teacher put incentives in the path of the pupil, ideas and feelings that prompt him to self-denial?

Interest as a source of *will-stimulus* has peculiar advantages. It is not desired that the inclinations and feelings shall get the mastery of the mind, certainly not the disorderly and momentary desires. Higher desires, indeed, should properly influence the will, as the desire of the approval of conscience, the desire to attain excellence, to gain strength and mastery, to serve others, etc. But the importance of awakening interest as a basis of will cultivation is found in the favorable mental state induced by interest as a preliminary to will action along the best lines. Interest is not an impetuous force like the desires, prompting to instant action, but a quiet, permanent undertone, which brings everything into readiness for action, clears the deck, and begins the attack. It would be a vast help to many boys and girls if the irksomeness of study in arithmetic or grammar, which is so fatal to will energy, could give way to the spur of interest, and when the wheels are once set in motion, progress would not only begin but be sustained by interest.

It is pretty generally agreed to by thoughtful educators, that in giving a child the broad foundations of education, we should aim not so much at knowledge as at capacity and *appreciation* for it. A universal receptivity, such as Rousseau requires of Emile, is a desideratum. Scarcely a better dowry can be bestowed upon a child by education, than a desire for knowledge and an intelligent interest in all important branches of study. Herbart's many-sided interest is to strengthen and branch out from year to year during school life, and become a permanent tendency or force in later years. No school can give even an approach to full and encyclopedic knowledge, but no school is so humble that it may not throw open the doors and present many a pleasing prospect into the fields of learning.

With Herbart, therefore, a many-sided, harmonious interest promotes *will-energy* through all the efforts of learning from childhood up, and when the work of general education has been completed, the youth is ready to launch out into the world with a strong, healthy appetite for information in many directions. The best fruitage of such a course will follow in the years that succeed school life. Interest is a very practical thing. It is that which gives force and momentum to ideas. It is not knowledge itself, but, like the invisible principle of life, it converts dead matter into living energy. In our schools thus far we have had too much faith in the mechanics of education. Too much virtue has been imputed to facts, to knowledge, to sharp tools. We have now to learn that *incentive* is a more important thing in education; that is, a direct, permanent, many-sided interest.

CHAPTER IV.

CONCENTRATION.

By concentration is meant such a connection between the parts of each study and such a spinning of relations and connecting links between different sciences that unity may spring out of the variety of knowledge. History, for example, is a series and collocation of facts explainable on the basis of cause and effect, a development. On the other hand, history is intimately related to geography, language, natural science, literature, and mathematics. It would be impossible to draw real history out by the roots without drawing all other studies out bodily with it. Is there then any reason why school history should ignore its blood relationships to other branches of knowledge?

Concentration is so bound up with the idea of *character-forming* that it includes more than school studies. It lays hold of *home influences* and all the experiences of life outside of school and brings them into the daily service of school studies. It is just as important to bind up home experience with arithmetic, language, and other studies as it is to see the connection between geography and history. In the end, all the knowledge and experience gained by a person at home, at school, and elsewhere should be classified and related, each part brought into its right associations with other parts.

Nor is it simply a question of throwing the varied sorts of *knowledge* into a network of crossing and interwoven series so that the person may have ready access along various lines to all his knowledge stores. Concentration draws the *feelings* and the *will* equally into its circle of operations. To imagine a character without feeling and will would be like thinking a watch without a mainspring. All knowledge properly taught generates feeling. The will is steadily laying out, during the formative period of education, the highways of its future ambitions and activities. Habits of willing are formed along the lines of associated thought and feeling. The more feeling and will are enlisted through all the avenues of study and experience, the more permanent will be their influence upon character.

In attempting to solve the problem of concentration the question has been raised whether a *single study*, the most important, of course, should constitute a concentrating nucleus, like the hub in a wheel, or whether *all studies* and *experience* are to be brought into an organic whole of related parts. It is evident that history and natural science at least hold a leading place among studies and determine to some extent the selection of materials in reading and language lessons.

The *center* for concentrating efforts in education is not so much the knowledge given in any school course as the *child's mind* itself. We do not desire to find in the school studies a new center for a child's life so much as the means for fortifying that original stronghold of character which rests upon native mental characteristics and early home influences. We have in mind not the objective unity of different studies considered as complete and related sciences, nor any general model to which each mind is to be conformed, but the practical union of all the experiences and knowledge that find entrance into a particular mind.

The *unity of the personality* as gradually developed in a child by wise education is essential to strength of character. Ackerman says on this point, ("Ueber Concentration," p. 20.) "In behalf of character development, which is the ultimate aim of all educative effort, pedagogy requires of instruction that it aid in forming the *unity of the personality,* the most primitive basis of character. In requiring that the unity of the personality be formed it is presupposed that this unity is not some original quality, but something to be first developed. It remains for psychology to prove this and to indicate in what manner the unity of the personality originates. Now, psychology teaches that the personality, the ego, is not something original, but something that must be first developed and is also changeable and variable. The ego is nothing else than a psychological phenomenon, namely, the consciousness of an interchange between the parts of an extensive complex of ideas, or the reference of all our ideas and of the other psychical states springing out of them to each other. Experience teaches this. In infancy the ego, the personality, is consciously realized in one person sooner, in another later. In the different ages of life, also, the personality possesses a different content. The deeper cause for the mutual reference of all our manifold ideas to each other and for their union in a single point, as it were, may be found in the *simplicity of the soul,* which constrains into unity all things that are not dissociated by hindrance or contradiction. The soul, therefore, in the face of the varied influences produced by contact with nature and society, is active in concentrating its ideas, so that with mental soundness as a basis, the ego, once formed, in spite of all the transitions through which it may pass, still remains the same."

There is then a natural *tendency* of the mind *to unify* all its ideas, feelings, incentives. On the other hand the knowledge and experiences of life are so varied and seemingly contradictory that a young person, if left to himself or if subjected to a wrong schooling, will seldom work his way to harmony and unity. In spite of the fact that the soul is a simple unit and tends naturally to unify all its contents, the common experience of life discovers in it unconnected and even antagonistic thought and knowledge-centers. People are sometimes painfully surprised to see how the same mind may be lifted by exalted sentiments and depressed by the opposite. The frequent examples that come to notice of men of superiority and virtue along certain lines, who give way to weakness and wrong in other directions, are sufficient evidence that good and evil may be systematically cultivated in the same character, and that instead of unity and harmony education may collect in the soul heterogeneous and warring elements which make it a battle ground for life. All such disharmony and contradiction lend inconsistency and weakness to character. Not only can incompatible lines of thought and of moral action become established in the same person, but even those studies which could be properly harmonized and unified by education may lie in the mind so disjointed and unrelated as to render the person awkward and helpless in spite of much knowledge. In unifying the various parts of school education, and in bringing them into close connection with children's other experiences, the school life fulfills one of its chief duties.

Among other things tending toward consistency of character there must be *harmony between the school and home* life of a child. At home or among companions, perhaps unknown to the teacher, a boy or girl may be forming an habitual tendency and desire, more powerful than any other force in his life, and yet at variance with the best influence of the school. If possible the teacher should draw the home and school into a closer bond so as to get a better grasp of the situation and of its remedy. The school will fail to leave an effective impress upon such a child unless it can get a closer hold upon the sympathies and thus neutralize an evil tendency. It must league itself with better home influences so as to implant its own impulses in home life. How to unify home and school influences is one of those true and abiding problems of education that appeals strongly and sympathetically to parents and teachers.

Concentration evidently involves a solution of the question as to the relative value of studies. All the light that the discussion of *relative values* can furnish will be needed in selecting the different lines of appropriate study and in properly adjusting them to one another. The theory of *interest* will also aid us in this field of investigation.

Accepting therefore the results of the two preceding chapters, that history (in the broad sense) is the study which best cultivates moral dispositions; secondly, that natural science furnishes the indispensable insight into the external world, man's physical environment; and, thirdly, that language, mathematics, and drawing are but the formal side and expression of the two realms of real knowledge, we have the *broad outlines* of any true course of education. In more definitely laying out the parts of this course the natural interests and capacities of children in their successive periods of growth must be taken into the reckoning. When a course of study has been laid out on this basis, bringing the three great threads or cables of human knowledge into proper juxtaposition at the various points, we shall be ready to speak of the manner of really executing the plan of concentration.

Even after the general plan is complete and the studies arranged, the real work of concentration consists in *fixing the relations* as the facts are learned. Concentration takes for granted that the facts of knowledge will be acquired. It is but half the problem to learn the facts. The other half consists in understanding the facts by fixing the relations. Most teachers will admit that each lesson should be a collection of connected facts and that every science should consist of a series of derivative and mutually dependent lessons. And yet the study and mastery of arithmetic as a connection of closely related principles is not generally appreciated. With proper reflection it is not difficult to see that the facts of a single study like grammar or botany should stand in close serial or causal relation. If they are seen and fixed with a clear insight into these connections, by touching the chain of associations at any point one may easily bring the whole matter to remembrance.

Concentration, however, is chiefly concerned with the *relation of different studies* to each other. In this larger sense of an intimate binding together of all studies and experience into a close network of interwoven parts, concentration is now generally ignored by the schools. In fact it would almost seem as if the purpose of teachers were to make a clear separation of the different studies from one another and to seal up each one in a separate bottle, as it were. The *problem* appears in two phases: 1. Taking the school studies as they now are, is it desirable to pay more attention to the natural connections between such studies as reading, geography, history, and language, to open up frequent communicating avenues between the various branches of educational work? 2. Or if concentration is regarded as still more important, shall the subject matter of school studies be rearranged and the lessons in different branches so adjusted to each other that the number of close relations between them may be greatly increased? Then with the intentional increase of such connecting links would follow a more particular care in fixing them. We have assumed the latter position, and claim that the whole construction of the school course and the whole method of teaching should contribute powerfully to the *unification* of all the knowledge and experience in each child's mind.

Without laying any undue stress upon simple knowledge, we believe that a small amount of well articulated knowledge is more valuable than a large amount of loose and fragmentary information. A small, disciplined police force is able to cope with a large, unorganized mob. "The very important principle here involved is that the value of knowledge depends not only upon the *distinctness* and *accuracy* of the ideas, but also upon the *closeness and extent of the relations* into which they enter. This is a fundamental principle of education. It was Herbart who said, 'Only those thoughts come easily and frequently to the mind which have at some time made a strong impression and which possess numerous connections with other thoughts.' And psychology teaches that those ideas which take an isolated station in the mind are usually weak in the impression they make, and are easily forgotten. A fact, however important in itself, if learned without reference to other facts, is quite likely to fade quickly from the memory. It is for this reason that the witticisms, sayings, and scattered pieces of information, which we pick up here and there, are so soon forgotten. There is no way of bringing about their frequent reproduction when they are so disconnected, for the reproduction of ideas is largely governed by the law of association. One idea reminds us of another closely related to it; this of another, etc., till a long series is produced. They are bound together like the links of a chain, and one draws another along with it just as one link of a chain drags another after it. A mental image that is not one of such a series cannot hope to come often to consciousness; it must as a rule sink into oblivion, because the usual means of calling it forth are wanting." (F. McMurry, "Relation of natural science to other studies.")

We are not conscious of the constant dependence of our thinking and conversation upon the *law of association*. It may be frequently observed in the familiar conversation of several persons in a company. The simple mention of a topic will often suggest half a dozen things that different ones are prompted to say about it, and may even give direction to the conversation for a whole evening. Now if it is true that ideas are more easily remembered and used if associated, let us *increase the associations*. Why not bind all the studies and ideas of a child as closely together as possible by natural lines of association? Why not select for reading lessons those materials which will throw added light upon contemporaneous lessons in history, botany, and geography? Then if the reading lesson presents in detail the battle of *King's Mountain*, take the pains to refer to this part of the history and put this lesson into connection with historical facts elsewhere learned. If a reading lesson gives a full description of the *palm tree*, its growth and use, what better setting could this knowledge find than in the geography of Northern Africa and the West Indies?

The numerous associations into which ideas enter, without producing confusion make them more *serviceable* for every kind of use. "It is only by associating thoughts closely that a person comes to possess them securely and have command over them. One's reproduction of ideas is then rapid enough to enable him to comprehend a situation quickly, and form a judgment with some safety; his knowledge is all present and ready for use; while on the other hand, one whose related thoughts have never been firmly welded together reproduces slowly, and in consequence is wavering and undecided. His knowledge is not at his command and he is therefore weak." (F. McMurry.) The greater then the number of clear mental relations of a fact to other facts in the same and in other studies the more likely it is to render instant *obedience* to the will when it is needed. Such ready mastery of one's past experiences and accumulations promotes confidence and power in action. Concentration is manifestly designed to give strength and decision to character. But a careless education by neglecting this principle, by scattering the mind's forces over broad fields and by neglecting the connecting roads and paths that should bind together the separate fields, can actually undermine force and decision of character.

In later years when we consider the *results of school methods* upon our own character we can see the weakness of a system of education which lacks concentration, a weakness which shows itself in a lack of *retentiveness* and of ability to use acquired knowledge. We are only too frequently reminded of the loose and scrappy state of our acquired knowledge by the ease with which it eludes the memory when it is needed. To escape from this disagreeable consciousness in after years, we begin to spy out a few of the mountain peaks of memory which still give evidence of submerged continents. Around these islands we begin to collect the wreckage of the past and the accretions of later study and experience. A thoughtful person naturally falls into the habit of collecting ideas around a few centers, and of holding them in place by links of association. In American history, for instance, it is inevitable that our knowledge becomes congested in certain important epochs, or around the character and life of a few typical persons. The same seems to be true also of other studies, as geography and even geometry. The failure to acquire proper *habits of thinking* is also exposed by the experience of practical life. In life we are compelled to see and respect the causal relations between events. We must calculate the influences of the stubborn forces and facts around us. But in school we often have so many things to learn that we have no time to think. At least half the meaning of things lies not in themselves, but in their relations and effects. Therefore, to get ideas without getting their significant relations, is to encumber the mind with ill-digested material. A sensible man of the world has little respect for this kind of learning.

One reason why knowledge is so poorly understood and remembered is because its *real application* to other branches of knowledge, whether near or remote, is so little observed and fixed. Looking back upon our school studies we often wonder what botany, geometry, and drawing have to do with each other and with our present needs. Each subject was so compactly stowed away on a shelf by itself that it is always thought of in that isolation,—like Hammerfest or the Falkland Islands in geography,—out of the way places. Are the various sciences so distinct and so widely separated in nature and in real life as they are in school? An observant boy in the woods will notice important relations between animals and plants, between plants, soil, and seasons that are not referred to in the text-books. In a carpenter shop he will observe relations of different kinds of wood, metals, and tools to each other that will surprise and instruct him. In the real life of the country or town the objects and materials of knowledge, representing the sciences of nature and the arts of life, are closely jumbled together and intimately dependent upon each other. The very closeness of causal and local connections and the lack of orderly arrangement shown by things in life make it necessary in schools to classify and arrange into sciences. But it is a vital mistake to suppose that the knowledge is complete when classified and learned in this scientific form. Classification and books are but a faulty means of getting a clear insight into nature and human life or society. Knowledge should not only be mastered in its scientific classifications but also constantly referred back to things as seen in practical life and closely traced out and fixed in those connections. The vital connections of different studies with each other are best known and realized by the study of nature and society.

In later life we are convinced at every turn of the need of being able to recognize and use knowledge *outside of its scientific connections*. A lawyer finds many subjects closely mingled and causally related in his daily business which were never mentioned together in textbooks. The ordinary run of cases will lead him through a kaleidoscope of natural science, human life, commerce, history, mathematics, literature, and law, not to speak of less agreeable things. But the same is true of a physician, merchant, or farmer, in different ways. Shall we answer to all this that schools were never designed to teach such things? They belong to professions or to the school of life, etc.

But it is not simply in professions and trades that we find this close mingling and dependence of the most divergent sorts of knowledge, this unscientific mixing of the sciences. Everywhere knowledge, however well classified, is one-sided and misleading, which does not conform to the conditions of real life. A wise *mother* in her household has a variety of problems to meet. From cellar to garret, from kitchen to library, from nursery to drawing-room, her good sense must adapt all sorts of knowledge to real conditions. In bringing up her children she must understand physical and mental orders and disorders. She must judge of foods and cooking, of clothing, as to taste, comfort, and durability; of the exercises and employments of children, etc. Whether she is conscious of it or not, she must mingle a knowledge of chemistry, psychology, physiology, medicine, sanitation, the physics of light and air, with the traditional household virtues in a sort of universal solvent from which she can bring forth all good things in their proper time and place. As Spencer says, education should be a preparation for complete living; or, according to the old Latin maxim, we learn *non scholae sed vitae*. The final test of a true mastery and concentration of knowledge in the mind is the ability to use it readily in the varied and tangled relations of actual experience.

We are accustomed to take refuge behind the so-called "mental discipline" that results from studies, whether or not anything is remembered that bears upon the relations of life. There are doubtless certain formal habits of mind that result from study even though, like Latin, it is cast aside as an old garment at the end of school days. Transferring our argument then to this ground, is there any "habit of thinking" more valuable than that *bent of mind* which is not satisfied with the mere memorizing of a fact but seeks to interpret its value by judging of its influence upon other facts and their influence upon it? No subject is understood by itself nor even by its relation to other facts in the same science, but by its relation to the whole field of knowledge and experience. Unless it can be proven that the study of relations is above the school-boy capacity, it is doubtful if there is any mental habit so valuable at the close of school studies as the disposition to *think* and *ponder*, to trace relations. The relations which are of interest and vital importance are those which in daily life bind all the realms of science into a network of causally connected parts.

The multiplication of studies in the common school in recent years will soon compel us to pay more attention to concentration or the mutual relation of knowledges. There is a resistless tendency to convert the course of studies into an *encyclopedia* of knowledge. To perceive this it is only necessary to note the new studies incorporated into the public school within a generation. Drawing, natural science, gymnastics, and manual training are entirely new, while language lessons, history, and music have been expanded to include much that is new for lower grades. Still other studies are even now seeking admission, as modern languages, geometry, and sewing. In spite of all that has been said by educational reformers against making the acquisition of knowledge the basis of education, the range and variety of studies has been greatly extended and chiefly through the influence of the reformers. This expansive movement appears in schools of all grades. The secondary and fitting schools and the universities have spread their branches likewise over a much wider area of studies. We are in the full sweep of this movement along the whole line and it has not yet reached its flood.

The *simplicity* of the old course both in the common school and in higher institutions is in marked contrast to the present multiplicity. It was a narrow current in which education used to run, but it was deep and strong. In higher institutions the mastery of Latin and of Latin authors was the *sine qua non*. In the common school arithmetic was held in almost equal honor. Strong characters have often been developed by a narrow and rigid training along a single line of duty as is shown in the case of the Jesuits, the Humanists, and the more recent devotees of natural science.

As contrasted with this, the most striking feature of our public schools now is their *shallow and superficial* work. It is probable that the teaching in lower grades is better than ever before, but as the tasks accumulate in the higher grades there is a great amount of smattering. The prospect is, however, that this disease will grow worse before a remedy can be applied. The first attempt to cultivate broader and more varied fields of knowledge in the common school must necessarily exhibit a shallow result. Teachers are not familiar with the new subjects, methods are not developed, and the proper adjustments of the studies to each other are neglected. No one who is at all familiar with our present status will claim that drawing, natural science, geography, and language are yet properly adjusted to each other. The task is a difficult one, but it is being grappled with by many earnest teachers.

It is obvious that the first serious effort to *remedy* this shallowness will be made by deepening and intensifying the culture of the new fields. The knowledge of each subject must be made as complete and detailed as possible. Well-qualified teachers and specialists will of course accomplish the most. They will zealously try to teach all the important things in each branch of study. But where is the limit? The capacity of children! And it will not be long before philanthropists, physicians, reformers, and all the friends of mankind will call a decisive halt. Children were not born simply to be stuffed with knowledge, like turkeys for a Christmas dinner.

It appears, therefore, that we must steer between Scylla and Charybdis, or that we are in a first-class educational *dilemma*. This conviction is strengthened by the reflection that there is no escape from fairly facing the situation. Having once put our hand to the plow we can not look back. The common school course has greatly expanded in recent years and there is no probability that it will ever contract. It has expanded in response to proper universal educational demands. For we may fairly believe that most of the studies recently incorporated into the school course are essential elements in the education of every child that is to grow up and take a due share in our society. It is too late to sound the retreat. The educational reformers have battled stoutly for three hundred years for just the course of study that we are now beginning to accept. The edict can not be revoked, that every child is entitled to an harmonious and equable development of all its human powers, or as Herbart calls it, a harmonious culture of many-sided interests. The nature of every child imperatively demands such broad and liberal culture, and the varied duties and responsibilities of the citizen make it a practical necessity. No narrow, one-sided culture will ever equip a child to act a just part in the complex social, political, and industrial society of our time. But the demand for *depth* of knowledge is just as imperative as that for *comprehensiveness*.

It is clear that two serious *dangers* threaten the quality of our education: First, loose and shallow knowledge; second, overloading with encyclopedic knowledge. What can concentration do to remedy the one and check the other? The *cure* for these two evils will be found in so adjusting the studies to each other, in so building them into each other, as to secure a mutual support. The study of a topic not only as it is affected by others in the same subject, but also by facts and principles in other studies, as an antidote against superficial learning. In tracing these causal relations, in observing the resemblances and analogies, the interdependence of studies, as geography, history, and natural science, a thoughtfulness and clearness of insight are engendered quite contrary to loose and shallow study.

Secondly, concentration at once discards the idea of encyclopedic knowledge as an aim of school education. It puts a higher estimate upon related ideas and a lower one upon that of complete or encyclopedic information. All the cardinal branches of education indeed shall be taught in the school, but only the *essential,* the *typical,* will be selected and an exhaustive knowledge of any subject is out of the question. Concentration will put a constant check upon over-accumulation of facts, and will rather seek to strengthen an idea by association with familiar things than to add a new fact to it. No matter how thorough and enthusiastic a specialist one may be, he is called upon to curtail the quantity of his subject and bring it into proper dependence upon other studies.

Historically considered the principle of concentration has been advocated and emphasized by many writers and teachers. The most striking and decided attempt to apply it was made by Jacotot in the first quarter of this century, and had great success in France. Mr. Joseph Payne, in interpreting Jacotot (Lectures on the Science and Art of Ed. p. 339), lays down as his main precept, *"Learn something thoroughly and refer everything else to it."* He emphasized above everything else *clearness* of insight and *connection* between the parts of knowledge. It was principally applied to the study of languages and called for perfect memorizing by incessant repetition and rigid questioning by the teacher to insure perfect understanding, in the first instance, of new facts acquired; and secondly, firm association with all previous knowledge. Jacotot and his disciples reached notable results by an heroic and consistent application of this principle and some of our present methods in language are based upon it. But on the whole the principle was only partially and mechanically applied. Its aim was primarily intellectual, even linguistic, not moral. There was no philosophical effort made to determine the relative value of studies and thus find out what study or series of studies best deserved to take the leading place in the school course. The importance of *interest,* as a means of rousing mental vigor and as a criterion for selecting concentrating materials suited to children at different ages, was overlooked.

A kind of concentration has long been practiced in Germany and to a considerable extent in our own schools which is known as the *concentric circles.*

In our schools it is illustrated by the treatment of geography, grammar, and history. In beginning the study of geography in the third or fourth grade it has been customary to outline the whole science in the first primary book. The earth as a whole and its daily and yearly motion, the chief continents and oceans, the general geographical notions, mountain, lake, river, etc., are briefly treated by definition and illustration. Having completed this general framework of geographical knowledge during the first year, the second year, or at least the second book, takes up the *same round of topics* again and enters into a somewhat fuller treatment of continents, countries, states, and political divisions. The last two years of the common school may be spent upon a large, complete geography; which, with larger, fuller maps and more names, gives also a more detailed account of cities, products, climate, political divisions, and commerce. Finally, physical geography is permitted to spread over much the same ground from a natural-science standpoint, giving many additional and interesting facts and laws concerning zones, volcanoes, ocean-beds and currents, atmospheric phenomena, geologic history, etc. The same earth, the same lands and oceans, furnish the outline in each case, and we travel over the same ground three or four times successively, each time adding new facts to the original nucleus. There is an old proverb that "repetition is the mother of studies," and here we have a systematic plan for repetition, extending through the school course, with the advantage of new and interesting facts to add to the grist each time it is sent through the mill. It is an attractive plan at first sight, but if we appeal to experience, are we not reminded rather that it was dull repetition of names, boundaries, map questions, location of places, etc., and after all not much detailed knowledge was gained even in the higher grades? Again, is it not contrary to reason to begin with definitions and general notions in the lower grades and end up with the interesting and concrete in the higher?

In language lessons and grammar it has been customary to learn the kinds of sentence and the parts of speech in a simple form in the third and fourth grades and in each succeeding year to review these topics, gradually enlarging and expanding the definitions, inflections, and constructions into a fuller etymology and syntax. In United States history we are beginning to adopt a similar plan of repetitions, and the frequent reviews in arithmetic are designed to make good the lack of thoroughness and mastery which should characterize each successive grade of work. The course of religious instruction given in European schools is based upon the same reiteration year by year of essential religious ideas. The whole plan, as illustrated by different studies, is based upon a successive enlargement of a subject in concentric circles with the implied constant repetition and strengthening of leading ideas. A framework of important notions in each branch is kept before the mind year after year, repeated, explained, enlarged, with faith in a constantly increasing depth of meaning. There is no doubt that under good teaching the principle of the concentric circles produces some excellent fruits, a mastery of the subject, and a concentration of ideas within the limits of a single study.

The disciples of Herbart, while admitting the merits of the concentric circles, have subjected the plan to a severe *criticism*. They say it begins with general and abstract notions and puts off the interesting details to the later years, while any correct method with children will take the interesting particulars first, will collect abundant concrete materials, and by a gradual process of comparison and induction reach the general principles and concepts at the close. It inevitably leads to a dull and mechanical repetition instead of cultivating an interesting comparison of new and old and a thoughtful retrospect. It is a clumsy and distorted application of the principle of apperception, of going from the known to the unknown. Instead of marching forward into new fields of knowledge with a proper basis of supplies in conquered fields, it gleans again and again in fields already harvested. For this reason it destroys a proper interest by hashing up the same old ideas year after year. Finally the concentric circles are not even designed to bring the different school studies into relation to each other. At best they contribute to a more thorough mastery of each study. They leave the separate branches of the course isolated and unconnected, an aggregation of unrelated thought complexes. True concentration should leave them an organic whole of intimate knowledge-relations, conducing to strength and unity of character.

There is a growing conviction among teachers that we need a closer *articulation* of studies with one another. The expansion of the school course over new fields of knowledge and the multiplication of studies already discussed compels us to seek for a simplification of the course. A hundred years ago, yes, even fifty years ago, it was thought that the extension of our territory and government to the present limits would be impossible. It was plainly stated that one government could never hold together people so widely separated. Mr. Fiske says: (The Critical Period of Am. Hist., p. 60) "Even with all other conditions favorable, it is doubtful if the American Union could have been preserved to the present time without the railroad. Railroads and telegraphs have made our vast country, both for political and for social purposes, more snug and compact than little Switzerland was in the middle ages or New England a century ago." The analogy between the realm of government and of knowledge is not at all complete but it suggests at least the change which is imperatively called for in education. In education as well as in commerce there must be trunk lines of thought which bring the will as monarch of the mind into close communication with all the resources of knowledge and experience. Indeed in the mind of a child or of an adult there is much stronger necessity for centralization than in the government and commerce of a country. The will should be an undisputed monarch of the whole mental life. It is the one center where all lines of communication meet. London is not so perfect a center for the commerce and finance of England as is the conscious *ego* (smaller than a needle's point) for all its forms of experience.

Besides the central trunk lines of knowledge in history and natural science there are branches of study which are *tributary* to them, which serve also as connecting chains between more important subjects. Reading, for instance, is largely a relative study. Not only is the art of reading merely a preparation for a better appreciation of history, geography, arithmetic, etc., but even the subject-matter of reading lessons is now made largely tributary to other studies. The supplementary readers consist exclusively of interesting matter bearing upon geography, history, and natural science. It is a fact that reading is becoming more and more a relative study, and selections are regularly made to bear on other school work. Geography especially serves to establish a network of connections between other kinds of knowledge. It is a very important supplement to history. In fact history cannot dispense with its help. Geography lessons are full of natural science, as with plants, animals, rocks, climate, inventions, machines, and races. Indeed there are few if any school studies which should not be brought into close and important relations to geography. Again the more important historical and scientific branches not only receive valuable aid from the tributary studies but they abundantly supply such aid in return. Language lessons should receive all their subject-matter from history and natural science. While the language lessons are working up such rich and interesting materials for purposes of oral and written language, the more important branches are also illustrated and enriched by the new historical and scientific subjects thus incidentally treated.

An examination of these mutual relations and courtesies between studies may discover to us the fact that we are now unconsciously or thoughtlessly *duplicating* the work of education to a surprising extent. For example, by isolating language lessons and cutting them off from communication with history, geography, and natural science, we make a double or triple series of lessons necessary where a single series would answer the purpose. Moreover, by excluding an interesting subject-matter derived from other studies, the interest and mental life awakened by language lessons are reduced to a minimum. Interest is not only awakened by well selected matter taken from other branches but the relationships themselves between studies, whether of cause and effect as between history and geography, or of resemblance as between the classifications in botany and grammar—the relations themselves are matters of unusual interest to children.

Many teachers have begun to realize in some degree the value of these relations, their effect in enlivening studies, and the better articulation of all kinds of knowledge in the mind. But as yet all attempts among us to properly relate studies are but weak and ineffective approaches toward the solution of the great problem of concentration. The links that now bind studies together in our work are largely accidental and no great stress has been laid upon their value, but if concentration is grappled with in earnest it involves *relations at every step*. Not only are the principal and tributary branches of knowledge brought into proper conjunction, but there is constant forethought and afterthought to bring each new topic into the company of its kindred, near and remote. The mastery of any topic or subject is not clear and satisfactory till the grappling hooks that bind it to the other kinds of knowledge are securely fastened.

Concentration on a large scale and with consistent thoroughness has been attempted in recent years by the scholars and teachers of the *Herbart school*. It is based upon moral character as the highest aim, and upon a correlation of studies which attributes a high moral value to historical knowledge and consequently places a series of historical materials in the center of the school course. The ability of the school to affect moral character is not limited to the personal influence of the teacher and to the discipline and daily conduct of the children; but instruction itself, by illustrating and implanting moral ideas, and by closely relating all other kinds of knowledge to the historical series, can powerfully affect moral tendency and strength. If historical matter of the most interesting and valuable kind be selected for the central series, and the natural sciences and formal studies be closely associated with it, there will be harmony and union between the culture elements of the school course.

The Culture Epochs.

The problem that confronts us at the outset, when preparing a plan of concentration, is *how to select* the best historical (moral educative) materials, which are to serve as the central series of the course. The *culture epochs* (cultur-historische

Stufen) are, according to the Herbartians, the key to the situation. (This subject was briefly discussed under *Interest*.)

According to the theory of the *culture epochs*, the child, in its growth from infancy to maturity, is an epitome of the world's history and growth in a profoundly significant sense for the purpose of education. From the earliest history of society and of arts, from the first simple family and tribal relations, and from the time of the primitive industries, there has been a series of upward steps toward our present state of culture (social, political, and economic life). Some of the periods of progress have been typical for different nations or for the whole race; for example, the stone age, the age of barbarism, the age of primitive industries, the age of nomads, the heroic age, the age of chivalry, the age of despotism, the age of conquest, wars of freedom, the age of revolution, the commercial age, the age of democracy, the age of discovery, etc. What relation the leading epochs of progress in the race bear to the steps of change and growth in children, has become a matter of great interest in education. The assumption of the *culture epochs* is that the growth of moral and secular ideas in the race, represented at its best, is similar to their growth in children, and that children may find in the representative historical periods select materials for moral and intellectual nurture and a natural access to an understanding of our present condition of society. The culture epochs are those representative periods in history which are supposed to embody the elements of culture suited to train the young upon in their successive periods of growth. Goethe says, "Childhood must always begin again at the first and pass through the epochs of the world's culture." Herbart says, "The whole of the past survives in each of us;" and again, "The receptivity (of the child) changes continually with progress in years. It is the function of the teacher to see to it that these modifications advance steadily in agreement with these changes (in the world's history)." Ziller has attempted more fully to "justify this culture-historical course of instruction on the ground of a certain *predisposition* of the child's mental growth for this course." Again, "We are to let children pass through the culture development of mankind with accelerated speed." Herbart says, "The treasure of advice and warning, of precept and principle, of transmitted laws and institutions, which earlier generations have prepared and handed down to the latter, belongs to the strongest of psychological forces." That is, choice historical illustrations produce a weighty effect upon the minds of children, if selected from those epochs which correspond to a child's own periods of growth.

The culture epochs imply *an intimate union between history and natural science*, the two main branches of knowledge, at every step. The isolation between these studies, which has often appeared and is still strong, is unnatural and does violence to the unity of education historically considered. Men at all times have had physical nature in and around them. Every child is an intimate blending of historical and physical (natural science) elements. The culture epochs illustrate a *constant change and expansion of history and natural science* together and in harmony (despite the conflict between them). As men have progressed historically and socially from age to age their interpretation of nature has been modified with growing discovery, insight, invention, and utilization of her resources. Children also pass through a series of metamorphoses which are both physical and psychological, changing temper and mental tendency as the body increases in vigor and strength.

The culture epochs, by beginning well back in history, with those early epochs which correspond to a child's early years and tracing up the steps of progress in their origin and growth, pave the way for a clear insight into our present state of culture, which is a complex of historical and natural science elements. It is comparatively easy for us to see that to understand the present political, economic, and social conditions of the United States we are compelled to go back to the early settlements with their simple surroundings and slowly trace up the growth and increasing complexity of government, religion, commerce, manufactures, and social life. The theory of the culture epochs implies that the child began where primitive man began, feels as he felt, and advances as he advanced, only with more rapid strides; that as his physique is the hereditary outcome of thousands of years of history, and his physical growth the epitome of that development, so his mental progress is related to the mind progress of his ancestry. They go still further and assume that the subject-matter of the leading epochs is so well adapted to the changing phases and impulses of child life that there is a strong predisposition in children in favor of this course, and that the series of historical object lessons stirs the strongest intellectual and moral interests into life.

As a *theory* the culture epochs may seem too loose and unsubstantial to serve as the basis for such a serious undertaking as the education of children to moral character. There is probably no exact agreement as to what the leading epochs of the world's history are, nor of the true order of succession even of those epochs which can be clearly seen. The value of this theory is rather in its suggestiveness to teachers in their efforts to select suitable historical materials for children not in any exact order but approximately. So far as we are informed no one has yet tried to prove, in logical form, the necessary correspondence between the epochs of history and the periods of growth in children. It is rather an instinct which has been felt and expressed by many great writers. The real test of the value of this theory is not so much in a positive argument as in a general survey of the educational materials furnished by the historical epochs, and an experimental use of them in schools to see whether they are suited to the periods of child growth.

There are, however, certain *limits* to the theory of race progress that need to be drawn at once. It is easy to perceive that not all races have left such epochs behind them, because some are still in barbarism; others have advanced to a considerable height and then retrograded. Of those which have advanced with more or less steadiness for two thousand years, like England, France, and Germany, not every period of their history contains valuable culture elements. The great epochs are not clearly distinguishable in their origin and ending. Again, only those periods whose deeds, spirit, and tendency have been well preserved by history or, still better, have found expression in the work of some great poet or literary artist, can supply for children the best educative material.

The culture epochs of history can be of no service to us in schools except as they have been suitably *described* by able writers. In history and literature, as handed down to us by the great literary artists, many of the culture epochs have been portrayed by a master hand. In the Iliad, Homer gives us vivid and delightfully attractive scenes from life in the heroic age. The historical parts of the Old Testament furnish clear and classic expression to great typical historical scenes as illustrated in the lives of Abraham, Joseph, Moses, Joshua, David, and Solomon. The chief poets have expended a full measure of their art in presenting to posterity attractive events from striking epochs of the world's history. Homer, Virgil, Dante, Tennyson, and Longfellow have left for us such historical paintings as the Iliad, Odyssey, the Æneid, the Divine Comedy, Idyls of a King, Miles Standish, etc. Some of the best historians also have described such epochs of history in scarcely less attractive form. Xenophon's Anabasis, Livy's Punic Wars, Plutarch's Lives, Cæsar's Gallic Wars, the best biographies of Charlemagne, Columbus, Luther, Cromwell, Washington, are designed to give us a clear view of some of the great typical characters and events of history. Some of the leading novelists and imaginative writers in prose have performed a like service. Hypatia, Ivanhoe, Last Days of Pompeii, Romola, Uarda, and Robinson Crusoe are examples. The story of Siegfried, of King Arthur, of Bayard, of Tell, of Bruce, of Alfred, and the heroic myths of Greece, all bring out representative figures of the mythical age.

The typical epochs of the world's struggle and progress are reflected, therefore, in the *literary masterpieces* of great writers, whether poets, historians, biographers, or novelists. The simplest and choicest of these literary and historical ma terials, selected, arranged, and adapted for children, have been regarded by some thinkers as the strongest and best meat that can be supplied to children during their periods of growth. The history of each nation that has had a progressive civilization contains some such elements and masterpieces. It would be fortunate for each nation if it could find first in its own history all such leading epochs and corresponding materials. Then it could draw upon the historical and literary resources of other countries to complete and round out the horizon of thought.

Since the best materials selected from history are calculated to build a strong foundation of moral ideas and sentiments, this carefully selected *historical series* of studies has been chosen as the basis for a concentration of all the studies of the school course. Ziller, as a disciple of Herbart, was the first to lay out a course of study for the common school with history materials as a central series, based upon the idea of the culture epochs. Since religious instruction drawn from the Old and New Testament has always been an important study in German schools, he established a double historical series. The first was scriptural, representing the chief epochs of Jewish and Christian history from the time of Abraham to the Reformation; the second was national German history from the early traditional stories of Thuringia and the Saxon kings down to the Napoleonic wars and the entry of Emperor William into Paris in 1871. It should be remarked that in the first and second grade religious instruction does not appear in regular form, but in devotional exercises, Christmas stories, etc. Fairy stories and Robinson Crusoe are the chief materials used in the first and second grades, so that the regular historical series begin in the third.

The two lines of religious and secular history are designed to illustrate for each grade corresponding epochs of national history, both Jewish and German.

The parallel series stand as follows:

Religious.	*Secular.*
1st Grade.	Fairytales.
2nd Grade.	Robinson Crusoe.
3d Grade. The patriarchs, Abraham, Joseph, Moses.	Stories of Thuringia.
4th Grade. Judges and Kings. Samuel, Saul, David, Solomon.	The Nibelungen Song, Siegfried.
5th Grade. Life of Christ.	Henry I., Charlemagne, Boniface, Armenius.
6th Grade. Life of Christ.	Teutonic migrations, Crusades, Attila, Barbarossa, Rudolph.
7th Grade. Life of Paul.	Discovery of America, Reformation, Thirty Years' War.
8th Grade. Life of Luther.	Frederick the Great, Wars against Napoleon, William I.

The above outline is Ziller's plan, modified by Professor Rein.

In each grade is selected a body of classical or choice historical materials, representing a great period of German as well as of Jewish or Christian life, and especially suited to interest and instruct children, while illustrating moral ideas and deepening moral convictions. The body of historical narrative selected for any one grade is calculated to form a *center* or nucleus for concentrating all the studies of that year. Reading, language, geography, drawing, music, and arithmetic largely spring out of and depend upon this historical center, while they are also bound to each other by many links of connection. A full course for the eight grades of the common school, with this double historical series as a nucleus, has been carefully worked out and applied by Professor Rein and his associates. It has been applied also with considerable success in a number of German schools.

This great undertaking has had to run the gauntlet of a severe *criticism*. Its fundamental principles, as well as its details of execution, have been sharply questioned. But a long-continued effort, extending through many years, by able and thoroughly-equipped teachers, to solve one of the greatest problems of education, deserves careful attention. The general theory of concentration, the selection and value of the materials, the previous history of method, and the best present method of treating each subject, with detailed illustrations, are all worked out with great care and ability.

The Jewish and German historical materials, which are made the moral-educative basis of the common school course by the Herbartians, can be of no service to us except by way of example. Neither sacred nor German history can form any important part of an American course of study. Religious instruction has been relegated to the church, and German history touches us indirectly if at all. The epochs of history from which American schools must draw are chiefly those of the

United States and Great Britain. France, Germany, Italy, and Greece may furnish some collateral matter, as the story of Tell, of Siegfried, of Alaric, and of Ulysses; but some of the leading epochs must be those of our own national history.

Has the *English-speaking race* in North America passed through a series of historical epochs which, on account of their moral-educative worth, deserve to stand in the center of a common school course? Is this history adapted to cultivate the highest moral and intellectual qualities of children as they advance from year to year? There are few, if any, single nations whose history could furnish a favorable answer to this question. The English in America began their career so late in the world's history and with such advantages of previous European culture that several of the earlier historical epochs are not represented in our country. But perhaps Great Britain and Europe will furnish the earlier links of a chain whose later links were firmly welded in America.

The *history of our country* since the first settlements less than three hundred years ago is by far the best epitome of the world's progress in its later phases that the life of any nation presents. On reaching the new world the settlers began a hand-to-hand, tooth-and-nail conflict with hard conditions of climate, soil, and savage. The simple basis of physical existence had to be fought for on the hardest terms. The fact that everything had to be built up anew from small beginnings on a virgin soil gave an opportunity to trace the rise of institutions from their infancy in a Puritan dwelling or in a town meeting till they spread and consolidated over a continent. In this short time the people have grown from little scattered settlements to a nation, have experienced an undreamed-of material expansion; have passed through a rapid succession of great political struggles, and have had an unrivaled evolution of agriculture, commerce, manufactures, inventions, education, and social life. All the elements of society, material, religious, political, and social have started with the day of small things and have grown up together.

There is little in our history to appeal to children below the fourth grade, that is, below ten years; but from the beginning of the fourth grade on, American history is rich in moral-educative materials of the best quality and suited to children. We are able to distinguish *four principal epochs*: 1. The age of pioneers, the ocean navigators, like Columbus, Drake, and Magellan, and the explorers of the continent like Smith, Champlain, LaSalle, and Fremont. 2. The period of settlements, of colonial history, and of French and Indian wars. 3. The Revolution and life under the Articles of Confederation till the adoption of the Constitution. 4. Self-government under the Union and the growth and strengthening of the federal idea. While drawing largely upon general history for a full and detailed treatment of a few important topics in each of these epochs, we should make a still more abundant use of the *biographical* and *literary* materials furnished by each. The concentration of school studies, with a historical series suggested by the culture epochs as a basis, would utilize our American history, biography, and literature in a manner scarcely dreamed of heretofore.

We shall attempt to illustrate briefly this concentration of studies about materials selected from one of the culture epochs. Take, for example, *the age of pioneers* from which to select historical subject-matter for children of the fourth and fifth grades. It comprehends the biographies of eminent navigators and explorers, pioneers on land and sea. It describes the important undertakings of Columbus, Magellan, Cabot, Raleigh, Drake, and others, who were daring leaders at the great period of maritime discovery. The pioneer explorers of New England and the other colonies bring out strongly marked characters in the preparatory stage of our earliest history. Smith, Champlain, Winthrop, Penn, Oglethorpe, Stuyvesant, and Washington are examples. In the Mississippi valley De Soto, La Salle, Boone, Lincoln, and Robertson, are types. Still farther west Lewis and Clarke, and the pioneers of California complete this historical epoch in a series of great enterprises. Most of them are pioneers into new regions beset with dangers of wild beasts, savages, and sickness. A few are settlers, the first to build cabins and take possession of land that was still claimed by red men and still covered with forests. The men named were leaders of small bands sent out to explore rivers and forests or to drive out hostile claimants at the point of the sword.

Any one who has tried the effect of these stories upon children of the fourth grade will grant that they touch a deep native *interest*. But this must be a genuine and permanent interest to be of educative value. The *moral quality* in this interest is its virtue. Standish, Boone, La Salle, and the rest were stalwart men, whose courage was keenly and powerfully tempered. They were leaders of men by virtue of moral strength and superiority. Their deeds have the stamp of heroism and in approving them the moral judgments of children are exercised upon noble material. These men and stories constitute an epoch in civilization because they represent that stage which just precedes the first form of settled society. In fact some of the stories fall in the transition stage, where men followed the plow and wielded the woodman's axe, or turned to the war-path as occasion required. In every part of the United States there has been such a period, and something corresponding to it in other countries. We are prepared to assume, therefore, that these historical materials arouse a strong interest, implant moral ideas, and illustrate a typical epoch. They are also very *real*. These men, especially the land pioneers, were our own predecessors, traversing the same rivers, forests, and prairies where we now live and enjoy the fruits of their hardihood and labor.

Let us suppose that such a historical series of stories has its due share of time on the school program and that the stories are properly presented by the teacher and orally reproduced by the pupils. Into what *relations* shall the other studies of the school enter to these historical materials? How shall language, reading, geography, natural science, and arithmetic be brought into the close relation to history required by the idea of concentration.

The oral reproduction of the stories by the children is the best possible *oral language* drill, while their partial written review is the basis of much of the regular *composition* work. Language lessons on isolated and unconnected topics can thus be entirely omitted. The element of interest will be added to oral and written language lessons by the use of such lively stories.

Reading is chiefly tributary to the historical series. Such selections should be made for reading lessons as will throw additional light upon pioneer history and its related geography. Descriptions of natural scenery and choice selections from our best historians, as Irving and Bancroft, describing events or men of this period, should be used for reading lessons. Especially the best literary selections are to be utilized, as the Landing of the Pilgrims, Webster's and Everett's orations at Plymouth, Evangeline and Hiawatha, Indian legends and life, Miles Standish, The Knickerbocker History, and some of the original papers and letters of the early settlers. Whatever poems or prose selections from our best literature are found to bear directly or indirectly upon pioneer events, will add much interest and beauty to the whole subject. A second series of reading materials for these grades would be those masterpieces and traditions of European literature, which are drawn from a corresponding pioneer epoch in those countries; for example, Siegfried in Germany, Alaric in Italy, and Ulysses in Greece. A selection of reading material along these lines would exhibit much variety of prose and poetry, history, and geography. Unity would be given to it by the spirit and labors of a typical age and an intimate relation to history at all points established.

Geography has an equally close relation to history stories. For these grades geography and history cover the same geographical regions. Instead of being totally isolated from each other they should be purposely laid out on parallel lines with interlacing topics. North America and the Atlantic ocean are the field of action in both cases. These maritime explorers opened up the geography of this hemisphere at its most interesting stage. No part of the Atlantic ocean or of its North American coasts was overlooked by the navigators. The climate, vegetation and people upon its islands and coasts were curious objects to European adventurers. The first pioneers surveyed the eastern coast and the adjacent interior of a new continent, with its bays, rivers, forests, and mountains. The stories themselves are not intelligible without full geographical explanations, and the personal interest in the narratives throws a peculiar charm upon the geography.

The *Mississippi valley* is a great field for both history and geography. It is one of the striking physical features of North America and the best of stories find their setting in this environment. Not a great river of this region but is the scene of one of the stories. The lakes and streams were the natural highways of the explorers and settlers. The mountains obstructed their way, presenting obstacles but not limits to their enterprise. The great forests housed their game, concealed their enemies, and had to be cut down to make space for their homes and cornfields. The prairies farther west were a camping ground for them as well as for the deer and buffalo. There are no important physical features of the great valley that are not touched more or less in detail by the stories. It is the work of the geography of this year to enlarge and complete the pictures suggested by the stories, to multiply details, to compare and arrange and to associate with these the facts of our present political and commercial geography.

The relation between history and geography is so intimate that it requires some pedagogical skill to determine which of the two should take the lead. But we have already adjudged the history to be by far the more important of the two. Its subject-matter is of greater intrinsic interest to children, and as it already stands in the commanding center of the school course, we are disposed to bring the geography lessons into close dependence upon it.

In these grades *natural science* or nature study form a necessary complement to the circle of historical and geographical topics treated. Many interesting natural-science subjects, suggested by history and geography, can not be dealt with satisfactorily in those studies; for example, the tobacco plant, the cactus, the deer, the hot springs, the squirrel, the mariner's compass. Natural science studies begin naturally with the home neighborhood, with its plants, trees, animals, rocks, inventions, and products. But having surveyed and learned many of these things at home in his earlier years, the child is prepared, when geography and history begin, to extend his natural-science information to the larger geographical regions.

The history stories and geography suggest a large number of *natural-science topics*, so that there is abundant choice of materials while remaining in close connection with those studies. The vegetable and animal life and products of the sea, suggested by the voyages, are fishes, dolphins, whales, sea-birds, shells. Other topics are the construction of ships, the mariner's compass, and astronomy. The stories of the land pioneers open up a still richer field of natural science study for the common schools. Among animals are the beaver, otter, squirrel, coon, bear, fox, wildcat, deer, buffalo, domestic animals, wild turkeys, ducks, pigeons, eagle, hawk, wild bees, cat-fish, sword-fish, turtle, alligator, and many more. Among native products and fruits are mentioned corn, pumpkins, beans, huckleberries, grapes, strawberries, cranberries, tobacco, pawpaw, mulberry, haw, plum, apple, and persimmon. Of trees are oak, hickory, walnut, cypress, pine, birch, beech, and others. Tools, instruments, and inventions are mentioned, with their uses, as guns, Indian weapons, compass, thermometer, barometer, boats, carpenter's tools; also, the uses of iron, lead, leather, and many of the simple arts and economies of life, such as weaving, tempering of metals, tanning, and cooking. The natural wonders of the country, such as falls, caves, hot-springs, canons, salt licks, plains, interior deserts, and salt lakes, kinds of rocks, soils, forests and other vegetation, the phenomena of the weather and differences in climate, are referred to. All these and other topics from the broad realm of nature are suggested, any of which may serve as the starting point for a series of science lessons.

How far the natural science lessons can *heed the suggestions* of history and geography and still follow out and develop important science principles, is one of the great problems for solution. It would seem that the large number of natural-science topics touched upon by the history, when increased by the variety of home objects in nature and by still others called up by the geography work of these years, would give sufficient variety to the natural science work of the same period. By omitting some of these topics and enlarging upon others, developing the notions of classes and principles so far as is desirable, the natural-science lessons may be made sufficiently scientific without losing the close relation to the central subject-matter for the year. There is no doubt but the science-lessons will add greatly to many topics suggested by the stories and will bring the whole realm of nature into close relation to history and geography.

The subjects thus far discussed, that may be brought into close relation to the central stories, are oral and written language, reading and literature, geography, and the natural sciences. The connection between these branches are numerous and strong at every step. *Drawing* has a very intimate and important relation to the objects described in history, natural science, arithmetic, and geography; while the *songs* learned should express in those poetic and rhythmic forms which appeal so strongly to the feelings, many of the noblest ideas suggested by travel, scenery, history, and the experiences of home life.

Arithmetic, finally, seems to stand like an odd sheep among the studies. It is certainly the least social of the common school branches. While avoiding all forced connection between arithmetic and other studies, we shall find some points where the relations are simple and clear. Children in the first grade should see numbers in the leaves, flowers, trees, and animals they study. At the beginning of the first grade this would be a good informal way of beginning numbers. The value of *objects* in first and second grade number is so great that it is only a question as to how far the objects suggested by other lessons may be used.

But we are speaking of concentration in the fourth and fifth grades. In the stories and in geography we deal with journeys up great rivers, with the height of mountains, with the extent of valleys and lakes, with regular forts, mounds, and enclosures, with companies and bodies of men, with railroads, cities, and agricultural products, and with many other topics which suggest excellent practical problems in arithmetic for these grades. All such careful arithmetical computations add clearness and definiteness to historical and geographical ideas. The natural sciences have been so little systematically taught in our common schools, that we are scarcely able to realize what connection may be made between them and arithmetic. We know that in the advanced study and applications of some of the natural sciences, mathematics is an essential part.

A brief retrospect will make it appear that the history stories, natural sciences, and geography, with the more formal studies, such as reading, language, and arithmetic, may be brought into a *close organic harmony*. Each of them depends upon and throws light upon the other; and while the connections are natural, not forced, there is a concentration upon the central historical and literary matter that makes moral character the highest aim of teaching.

Since real concentration is practically a new educational undertaking, it involves a number of *unsolved subordinate problems*; for instance, how far shall science lessons, grammar, and geography follow their own principles of selection, based on the nature and scientific arrangement of their materials, while keeping up the dependence upon and connections with the central subject. But if concentration is a true principle of education, it is evident that none of these problems can be solved until concentration has been agreed upon and made fundamental. In this case those teachers who are trying to lay out courses of study in geography, natural science, or history, without regard to the relation of studies to each other, will have most of their work to do over again.

A little reflection will convince us, perhaps, that a year's work thus concentrated will produce a much more powerful and lasting impression upon children than the loose aggregation of facts which is usually collected during a year's work. Not only will the moral effect be intensified, but the close dependence of each study upon the others will be perceptibly felt as valuable and stimulating to the children.

If now we can conceive of the eight grades of the common school as eight stages passing naturally from one to another, each a unit composed of a net-work of well related facts, but the epochs closely related to each other in a rising series, from childhood almost to maturity, or from the beginning of history up to the present state of culture, we shall be able also to think of education as a succession of powerful culture influences, that will bring the child to our present standpoint fully conscious of his duties and surroundings.

NOTE.—A careful criticism of the theory of the culture epochs is found in Lange's Apperception translated by the Herbart club, published by D. C. Heath, p. 110, etc.

CHAPTER V.

INDUCTION.

We are now prepared to inquire into the mind's method of approach to any and all subjects. We have considered the aim of education, the value of different subjects as helping toward that aim, the natural interests which give zest to studies, and finally the general plan of combining and relating topics so as to bring about unity of purpose and unity of matter in the mind. As a child enters upon the work of acquisition are there any regulatives to guide the process of learning?

Induction, or the *concept-bearing process*, shows the tendency of our minds to advance from the inspection of particular objects and actions to the understanding of general notions or concepts. The study and analysis of this process casts us forthwith into the midst of psychology, and calls for a knowledge of that succession and net-work of mental activities discussed in all the psychologies; sensation, discrimination, perception, analysis and synthesis, comparison, judgment, generalization or concept, reasoning. An inquiry into these mental activities, which are among the most important in psychology, is necessary as a basis of induction and of general method.

But even the more profound study of psychology does not necessarily give insight into correct methods of teaching. Many great psychologists have had little or no interest in teaching. Even eminent specialists in electricity and chemistry have not often been those to draw the immediate practical benefit from their studies. The application of psychology to the work of instruction constitutes a distinct field of inquiry and experiment. The output of the best experimental thinking in this direction may be called pedagogy.

The process of induction or concept-building leads the mind, as above indicated, through a series of different acts. We may first observe how far the mind is naturally inclined to follow this process, and whether it is a mark of healthy mental action in children and in adults. Later we may examine more closely the successive stages in the process itself.

To get at the *natural process* it is well to observe first the action of a *child's* mind. By analyzing a simple case of a farmer's child we may trace the mental steps in forming a general notion. So long as it has seen no barn except that on its father's farm, the word *barn* means to it only that particular object. But when it discovers that one of the neighbors has a similar building called a barn, it learns to put these different objects under one head, and the general notion *barn* as a building for horses, cattle, and feed, gradually rises in the mind. Long before the child is six years old (school age) it may have seen enough of such barns for the general notion to be distinctly formed. By observing different objects, by comparing and grouping similar things together, it has formed a general notion in a regular process of induction, and that without any help from teachers.

At two and three years of age, or as soon as a child begins to recognize and name new objects (because of their resemblance to things previously seen) this tendency to concept-building is manifest. Another illustration: The child has seen the family horse several times till the word horse becomes associated with that animal. While out walking it sees another horse, and pointing its finger says "horse." The memory of the first horse and the similarity calls forth the natural conclusion that this is a horse, though it may not be able to formulate the sentence. More horses are seen and compared till the word becomes the name of a whole class of animals. By a gradual process of observation, comparison, and judgment the word horse comes to stand for a large group of objects in nature.

A child's mind is naturally very *active* in detecting resemblances and in grouping similar objects together. It notices that there are certain people called women, others called men; that certain animals are called sheep, others cattle. One class of objects receives the name book, another stove, etc. The work of observing, comparing, and classifying is a perpetual operation in the child's active moods. In this way, what may appear at first as an interminable confusion or blur of objects in nature begins to fall into groups and classes with appropriate names. It is the child's own way of bringing order out of the apparent chaos of his surroundings. All this process of classification is natural and nearly unconscious, and results in a better understanding and interpretation of the things around him.

Observe next the work of an educated *adult*, and how he increases and arranges his knowledge. If he is an incipient dry-goods merchant he learns by sight and touch to detect the quality of goods. He compares and classifies his experiences and becomes in time an expert in judging textile fabrics. On the other hand he becomes acquainted by personal contact with various customers and learns how to classify and judge them both as buyers and as debtors.

If a *botanist* finds a new plant he examines its stem, leaves, root, flower, seed, and environment. While entering into these details he is also comparing it with familiar classes of plants. Finally, he is not satisfied till he can definitely locate it in his previous system. With every new plant that he discovers he travels over the whole road from the individual particulars to the general classes of his whole system. The merchant and the scientist follow out with painstaking care and industry the same course which was involuntarily taken by the child; namely, observation of particulars, comparing and grouping into classes. The same habit of mind may be observed in all people who are growing knowledgewards and who possess any thoughtful instincts. In building up concepts, especially with the adult, induction is constantly mingled with deduction. As fast as general notions are formed they are used to interpret new objects. As the amount of this organized and classified knowledge increases, we reason more and more deductively.

In acquiring knowledge along the line of induction, we are on the road to the solution of the *puzzle*, that nature puts to every child. To every infant, indeed, the world is an enormous riddle or puzzle, whose parts lie in fragments about him, waiting the operation of his curious and inventive mind toward the reconstruction of the whole. Endless variety and complexity confront us all in the beginning. There is indeed an order and classification of things in nature, but it does not appear on the surface, and for centuries men remained ignorant of the underlying harmony. Nature is full of valuable secrets, but they lie concealed from the careless eye. They are to be detected by prying deeper into individual facts, by putting a thing here and a thing there together, by pondering on the relationship of things to each other in their nature, appearance, and cause. It is a remarkable fact that we not only increase knowledge best by analyzing, comparing, and classifying objects, experience, and phenomena—even into old age—but that the deeper we penetrate into the individual qualities and inner nature of objects, the more we extend and classify our information, the simpler all the operations of nature become to our understanding. The surprising simplicity and unity of nature in her varied phenomena is one of the mature products of scientific study. The most scientific thinker, then, is only trying to reduce to a simple explanation the same puzzle which confronted the infant in its cradle. The problem is the same and the method similar.

It is plain that the process of classifying objects and phenomena in nature and in society is the *beginning of scientific knowledge*. A child begins to learn as soon as it notices the resemblances in things and arranges them into groups. It will appear later that the mind does not follow a strictly logical method in gaining its groups, that it falls into natural errors and misconceptions; but in spite of these eccentric movements, the general trend is toward classifications and toward the language symbols that express them. In this power to associate, classify, and symbolize the products of experience in words is seen the marked difference between man and the animals. The latter have little power to compare and generalize, that is, to think. On a still higher plane, the difference between a careless, loose observer and a well-trained scientific thinker is largely a difference in accuracy, in inductive and deductive processes.

The important thing for the teacher to determine is whether this inductive or concept-building tendency furnishes any *solid ground upon which to base the work of instruction*. Admitting that it is a natural process, common to both old and young in acquiring knowledge, perhaps it can be neglected because it will take care of itself. If it is self-active, needing no artificial stimulus, let it alone. On the contrary, if in a healthy pursuit of knowledge it brings the varied mental powers into a natural sequence where they will strengthen and support one another, it should be studied and used by teachers. It would be very commonplace to say that each of the faculties or activities involved in the inductive process should be disciplined and strengthened by school studies. There is but little difference of opinion on this subject, though some would lay more stress upon sense training, some on memory, some on reasoning. The ground for this general conviction is the notorious fact that with children every one of these acts, is performed in a *faulty and superficial manner*. The observations of children are very careless and unreliable. Even adults are extremely negligent and inaccurate in their observations of natural objects, persons, and phenomena. But the mental powers brought to bear in observation are simple and elementary. The exercise of higher mental powers, such as analysis, comparison, judgment, and reasoning, is prone to be still more accidental and erroneous.

Acknowledging then the necessity for training all these powers, how can it best be done? Not by delegating to each study the cultivation of one kind or set of mental activities, but by observing that *the same general process* underlies the acquisition of knowledge in each subject, and that all the kinds of mental life are brought into action in nearly every study. In short, the inductive process is a natural highway of human thought in every line of study, bringing all the mental forces into an orderly, successive, healthful activity. We may yet discover that the inductive process not only gives the key to an interesting method of mastering different branches of knowledge, but in developing mental activity it brings the various mental powers into a strong natural sequence.

One of the great ends of intellectual culture is gradually *to transform this careless, unconscious, inductive tendency in children into the painstaking and exact scrutiny of the student, and later of the specialist.*

Although the inductive process is a common highway of thought in all stages of intellectual growth from childhood to maturity, certain parts of the road are much more frequently traveled in childhood, and still others in youth and maturity. It is the work of pedagogy to adapt its materials to these *changing phases* of soul life in children. In the analysis of the inductive and deductive processes we desire to come at the solution of this problem.

Considered as a whole, there is a simple phase of the inductive process which is best explained by the terms absorption and reflection. It appears in the study of simple as well as of complex objects, and indicates clearly the fundamental rhythm of the mind in acquiring and elaborating its knowledge. This action of the mind is a shuttle-like movement, a constant running back and forth between two extremes, *absorption* and *reflection*. We will test this statement upon examples. When we are in the mood for learning let some new object, a *sawmill*, attract the attention. A quick general glance at the place and its surroundings tells us what it is. Now trace the operation of the mill as it draws up the logs singly from the rafts lying on the margin of the river and converts them into lumber. You observe first how the logs are carried up an inclined slide by means of an endless chain with hooks, into the mill. You examine this first piece of machinery and notice its mode of action. As the logs enter the upper story of the mill, they are thrown by heavy levers to either side and roll down toward the saws. Here is another piece of machinery in its proper place. Having been stripped of the loose pieces of bark, the logs are grasped by another set of iron hands, lifted firmly to the carriage and passed to the circular or band-saw, which takes off the side slabs and squares them for the gang-saw. The squared logs are then carried along over rollers and collected before the gang-saws. From two to four of them are clasped firmly together and then forced up against the teeth of the parallel group of saws, issuing from them as a batch of lumber. The boards are then passed on to a set of men at small circular saws, by whom they are sorted and the edges trimmed, while still others with trucks carry them to the yard for stacking.

Take note of the operation of the mind as it passes from one part of the machinery to another. Each part is first examined by itself to get its construction and method. Then its relation to what precedes and what follows is noted. Finally, in review you survey the whole process in its successive stages and understand each part and its relation to the whole and to the purpose of the mill. We might call this an analysis and synthesis of the process of making lumber, or in other words absorption and reflection. In the observation of such a complex piece of machinery as a large mill the mind swings back and forth many times between absorption in the study of parts and reflection upon their relation to each other.

Having examined the mill in detail and grasped its parts as a connected whole, the next step is to observe its relation to the river, to the rafts and rafting-boats, and further back to the pineries and logging-camps up the river. (Northern Minnesota and Wisconsin.) The occupations and sights along the Upper Mississippi and its head-waters, the pineries, and even the spring floods, are intimately connected, causally, with the saw-mills and lumber yards lower down. Or going in the opposite direction from the saw-mill, we follow the lumber till it is used in the various forms of construction. Some of it enters the planing-mills and is converted into moldings, finishing lumber, sashes, blinds, etc. In all forms it is loaded upon the cars, and shipped westward to be used in the construction of houses and bridges.

Before we get through with the line of thought engendered by observing the saw-mill, we have canvassed the whole lumber industry from the pineries to the plans of architects and builders in the actual work of construction. Not only has there been this progress of the mind from one object or machine to another of a *series* connected by cause and effect, but there has been also a constant tendency to pass from the individual machines of which the series is composed to the classes of which these objects are typical. A circular-saw or a gang-saw is each typical of a class of saws. The same is true of each part of the machinery, as well as of the saw-mill or planing-mill considered as a whole. Each of these objects, whether simple or complex, suggests others similar which we have observed or seen represented in pictures. Each part of the machinery in turn becomes the center of a set of comparisons leading from the concrete object in question to the general notion of the class to which it belongs. For example, the steam engine in a mill is typical of all stationary engines used for driving machinery. But the parts of the engine are also typical of similar parts in other engines and machines, as the drive-wheel, cylinder, boiler, etc.

In all these cases we become absorbed in one thing for a while, only to recover ourselves and to reflect upon the thing in its wider relations, either tracing out connections of cause and effect, as in a series of machines, or passing from the single example to the class of which it is typical. Absorption and reflection! The mind swings back and forth like a pendulum between these two operations. Herbart, who closely defined this process, called it the *mental act of breathing*, because of the constancy of its movement. As regularly as the air is drawn into the lungs and again expelled, so regularly does the mind lose itself in its absorption with objects only to recover itself and reflect upon them.

In the inspection of a large *printing press* in one of our newspaper publishing-houses we meet with a similar experience. The attention becomes centered upon the press for a close analysis and synthesis of its parts. The cogs, wheels, rollers, inking-plate, the chases for the type, the application of the power, the springs and levers, each part receives a close inspection, and the secret of its connection with other parts is sought for. There is a vigorous effort not only to understand each part but also the connection of the whole. The shuttle-like movement of the mind back and forth between the parts, absorbed for a moment, reflecting for a moment, continues until the complex mechanism is understood. When this process has been satisfactorily completed, we are ready to turn our minds again to the other objects and rooms of the printing establishment. The work of the compositors, setting up different kinds of type, the proof-reading, the editorial work, the reporters, all come in for a share of attention. The reporters lead us to the great world outside whose happenings are brought here for publication. On the other hand, following the distribution of papers as they issue from the press, we think of news-boys, news-stands, mail-service, railroads, and postoffices. But the inspection of a printing press also leads the thoughts in other directions and suggests other presses, great and small, in other times and places, other printing establishments, until the whole business of printing and publishing books and papers springs into the thought.

If we desire to understand clearly the business of publishing a newspaper, we must enter into an observation of the parts of the process from the collection of its news to its distribution by the mails and carriers. Besides noting these parts we must observe their causal connection with each other and the rôle that each plays in the economy of the whole. The causal series thus clearly outlined produces insight into an occupation, while every typical machine or appliance is one of a cross series intercepting the original series. The acquisition and assimilation of knowledge in different subjects will be found to exhibit the mental states of absorption and reflection as just illustrated. Observe the manner in which we study a poem. It is first read and interpreted sentence by sentence, glancing from verse to verse to get the connections. When the whole piece has been read and understood in its parts and connections, the suggested lines of thought are taken up and followed out in their wider applications. Take for example the "Burial of Moses," and in the proper analysis and study of the poem, such a process of absorption and reflection is observable. In tracing the biography of John Quincy Adams or of Alexander Hamilton, the facts of personal experience and action first absorb the attention from step to step in the study of his life. But reflection on the bearings of these personal events, upon contemporaries, and upon public affairs is noticed all along. The same mental process is observed in studying a battle in history, a sentence in grammar, a squirrel in natural history, or a picture in art.

The effect of such mental absorption and reflection is to build up *concepts*. Series of causally related parts are also formed, but each series in the end becomes a more complete complex concept; that is, a representative of many similar series. The inspection of one printing establishment suggests others which are brought into comparison till the general notion, publishing-house, is more clearly conceived. The same is true in the lumber trade. The concept lumber-business is not confined to Minneapolis or Chicago, but is common to the great lake region, Maine, Washington, Norway, and other countries. Concepts become more varied and complex with the advance of studies, and there is scarcely anything we learn by observation or reflection that does not ultimately illustrate and build up our concepts. The observation of even the miscellaneous objects in a large city leads to a variety of concepts, and in the end, by comparison, to the general notion, *city*.

How strong the concept-creating tendency of all experience and thought is, can be seen in the *words* of language. The processes of thought become petrified in language. All progress in knowledge and acquisition of new ideas is reflected in language by an increase of words. But an examination of words in common use will show that they are nearly all the names of concepts. Proper names are the principal exception. Every common noun, verb, adjective, adverb, and preposition is the name of a concept; for example, horse, beauty, to steal, running, over, early, yellow, grape, ocean, etc. To understand these concepts there must be somewhere a progress from the individual to the abstract, an induction from particulars to a general concept.

Abstract or general notions cannot be acquired at first hand without specific illustrations. Even where the deductive process is supposedly employed, a closer examination will uncover the concrete or individual illustrations in the background, and until these are reached the concept has no clear meaning. The *concrete examples*, whether introduced sooner or later by way of explanation, are the real basis of the understanding of the concept. It is customary to invert the inductive process and to drive it stern forwards through grammar, geography, and other studies. Take, for example, the word boomerang as it comes up in a geography or reading lesson. Webster's dictionary, which is recommended to children as a first resort in such difficulties, calls it "A remarkable missile weapon used by the natives of Australia." This gives a faint notion by using the familiar word *weapon*. The picture accompanying the word in the dictionary gives a more accurate idea because nearer the concrete. The best possible explanation would be a real boomerang thrown by a native South-Sea Islander. In the absence of these, a picture and a vivid description are the best means at our disposal. The common mistake is in learning and reciting the definition while neglecting the concrete basis. By way of further illustration, try to explain to children, who have never heard of them before, the egg-plant, palm-tree, cactus, etc.

It would be of interest to inquire into the process of concept-building in each of the *school studies*, where it appears under quite varying forms. The natural sciences are perhaps the best examples of concept-building from concrete materials, advancing regularly through a series of concepts from the individuals and species to the most general classes of plants, animals, etc. In chemistry and physics the laws and general principles are based on substances, experiments, and processes observable by the senses. Grammar and language, when studied as a science, advance from concept to concept through etymology and syntax. In geography and history the concepts are less definite and more difficult to formulate, and yet there are many typical ideas which are to be developed and illustrated in each of these studies; in history, for example, colony, legislature, governor, general, revolution, institutions and customs, political party, laws of development, causal relations, inventions, etc.; in geography, continents, oceans, forms of relief, kinds of climate and causes, occupations, products, commerce, etc. The fundamental truths and relations and rules of arithmetic must be developed from objects and illustrations. Reading, spelling, and writing are arts, not sciences, and are more concerned with skill in execution than with the acquisition of a body of scientific truths. And yet certain general truths are emphasized and applied in these studies.

Much needless confusion has been caused by raising the question *where to begin* in learning. Do we proceed from the whole, to the parts, or from the parts to the whole? In making the acquaintance of sense-objects it seems clear that we first perceive wholes (somewhat vaguely and indefinitely). The second impulse is to analyze this whole into its parts, then recombine them (synthesis) into a whole which is more definitely and fully grasped. A house, for example, is generally first perceived as a whole; and later it is examined more particularly as to its materials, rooms, stairways, conveniences, furnishings, etc. The same is true with a mountain, a butterfly, a man. Thus far we have proceeded from the whole to the parts and then back again; analysis and synthesis. The next movement is from this whole or object toward a group of similar objects, a class notion. By comparing one thing with others similar, a class notion is formed which includes them all. Each individual is a whole, but is also a type of the entire group. The general mental movement is successively in two directions from any particular object; first, from the whole to the parts, then grasping this whole in a richer, fuller sense, the mind seeks for relations which bind this object with others similar into a group, a more complex product, a concept. There may appear to be an exception to this rule in the case of a city, a continent, a railroad, or any concrete object so large and complex that it cannot be grasped by a single effort of sense perception. But even here it is usual with us first to represent the whole object to our thought by means of a sketch, map, or figure of speech, so as first to get a quick survey of the whole thing. In history, also, we first grasp at wholes, then enter into a detailed account of an event, a campaign, a voyage, a revolution, etc. There are many complex wholes in geography and history with which it is not wise to begin, because it requires a long and painful effort to get at the notion of the whole. The wholes we have in mind are those which can be almost instantly grasped. Not, for example, an outline of American history or of the world's history. The choice of suitable wholes with which to begin is based upon the child's interest and apperceptive powers.

Having thus examined into the general nature of the inductive process and the extent of its application to school studies and to other forms of acquiring knowledge, we are led to a closer practical discussion of each of the two chief stages of induction: First, *observation or intuition*; that is, the direct perception through the senses or through consciousness, of the realities of the external world and of the mind. Second, association of ideas with a view to generalizing and *forming concepts*.

Intuition[1] implies object lessons in a wide sense. By object lessons is usually meant things in nature perceived through the senses. But it is necessary to extend the idea of object lessons beyond the objects and phenomena of the physical world, to which it has been usually limited. It includes perception of our own mental states. These direct experiences of our own inner states are the primary basis of our understanding of other people's feelings, mental states, and actions. In short, an understanding of the phenomena of individual life, (the acts of persons) of society, and of history, is based upon a knowledge of our own feelings and mental acts, and upon the accuracy with which we have observed and interpreted similar things in other persons. We have already seen that a right appreciation of companions, biographies, social life, and history, is the strongest of psychological forces in its formative influence upon character. For this reason, also, history includes the first and most important body of school studies. But object lessons drawn from physical nature do not measurably qualify us for a better appreciation of individual and social life and action. The fundamental illustrative materials for history are drawn from another source, from the depth of the heart and inner experience of each person. Many words in our own school books can be illustrated and explained by objects and activities in physical nature, but a large part of the words in common use in our readers and school books can be explained by no external objects. They depend for their interpretation upon the child's own feelings, desires, joys, griefs, etc., and upon similar phenomena observed in others.

Object lessons in this liberal sense point to the direct exercise of the senses and intuitions in the acquisition of experience of all sorts. They include the objects, persons, and events that we see around us and our own experiences in ordinary life—the grass, plants, trees, and soils; the animals, wild and tame, with their structure, habits, and uses; the rocks, woods, hills, streams, seasons, clouds, heat, and cold. There is also the observation of devices and inventions; tools, machinery and their workings, the different raw and manufactured products, with their ways of growth and transformation. Besides these are the various kinds and dispositions of men, different classes and races of people, with great variety of character, occupation, and education. Their actions, modes of dress, and customs are included. But we have many other primary and indispensable lessons to learn from the playground, the street, from home and church, from city and country, from travel and sight seeing, from holidays and work days, from sickness, and healthful excursions. Even a child's own tempers, faults, and successes are of the greatest value to himself and to the teacher in a proper self-understanding and mastery. By object lessons, therefore, we mean all that a child becomes conscious of through the direct action of his senses and of his mind upon external nature or inner experience. It is desired that a child's knowledge in all direct experience be simple, clear, and according to the facts. All words that he uses become only signs

[1] Intuition is popularly used in a sense different from the above. We are in need of a word which has the same meaning as the German word, *Anschauung,* for which there is no popular equivalent in English. Intuition, as defined by Webster, is nearly the same: "direct apprehension, or cognition; immediate knowledge, as in perception or consciousness."

For a discussion of this term, see Quick's Educational Reformers, p. 361, Appleton's edition.

of the realities of his experience. Every word stands for a potent thought in his own life history. Of course object lessons in this rich and real sense can not be confined to such few objects—birds, leaves, models, and straws—as can be brought into a school room. All the world, especially the outside world, becomes

> "A complex Chinese toy
> Fashioned for a barefoot boy."

Many of the most interesting objects and phenomena in nature and of man's construction can not be observed in the school room at all, for instance, the river, the bridge, the forest, the flight of birds, the sunrise, the storm, the stars, etc. Still they must know these very things and know how to use them better in constructing the mind's treasures than they are wont to do. In reading, grammar, geography, arithmetic, and nature study, we desire to ground school discussions daily upon the clear facts of experience, of personal observation. We need to clear up all confused and faulty perceptions and to stimulate children to make their future observations more reliable.

We have already seen the importance of object lessons in this full and real sense to *interest*. Interest in every study is awakened and constantly reenforced by an appeal, not to books, but to life. Much of the dull work in arithmetic, geography, and other studies is due to the neglect of these real, illustrative materials.

Of the six great sources of interest, (Herbart's) three, the *empirical*, the *esthetic*, and the *sympathetic*, deal entirely with concrete objects or with individuals, while even the *speculative* and *social* interests are often based directly upon particular persons or phenomena. In addition to this it may be said that the interests of children are overwhelmingly with the concrete and imaginative phases of every subject, and only secondarily with general truths and laws. The latter are of greater concern to older children and adults. Object lessons therefore contain a life-giving element that should enter into every subject of study.

Nor should these interesting, illustrative object lessons be limited to the lower grades. They contain the combustible material upon which an abiding interest in any subject is to be kindled. There are indeed other and perhaps higher sources of interest, but they are largely dependent upon these original springs that flow from the concrete beginnings.

In the second place, object lessons supply a stock of *primary ideas* which form the foundation of all later progress in knowledge. This is not a question of interest merely, but of *understanding*, of capacity to get at the meaning of an idea. Concepts are not the raw materials with which the mind works, but they are elaborated out of the raw products furnished by the senses and other forms of intuition. As cloth is manufactured out of the raw cotton and wool produced on the farm or in southern fields, so concepts are a manufactured article, into whose texture materials previously gathered enter. Concepts do not grow up directly from the soil of the mind any more than ready-made clothing grows on bushes or on the backs of the wearers. Concepts must be made out of stuff that is already in the mind, as woolen blankets are spun and woven out of fleeces. Our present contention is that the mind shall be filled up with the best quality of raw stuff, otherwise there will be defect and deficiency in its later products. The stuff out of which concepts are built is drawn from the varied experiences of life. On account of this intimate relation between the realities of life and school studies they cannot be separated. Every branch, especially in elementary studies, must be treated concretely and be built up out of sense materials. Every study has its concrete side, its illustrative materials, its colors of individual things taken from life. Every study has likewise its more general scientific truths and classifications. The prime mistake in nearly all teaching and in the text-book method is in supposing that the great truths are accessible in some other way than through the concrete materials that lie properly at the entrance. The text-books are full of the abstractions and general formulæ of the sciences; but they can, in the very nature of the case, deal only in a meager way with the individual objects and facts upon which knowledge in different subjects is based. This necessary defect in a text-book method must be made good by excursions, by personal observation, by a constant reference of lessons to daily experience outside of school, by more direct study of our surroundings, by the teacher perfecting himself in this kind of knowledge and in its skillful use.

There was a current belief at one time that object lessons should form a *special study* for a particular period of school life, namely, the first years. It was thought that sufficient sense-materials could be collected in two or three years to supply the whole school curriculum. But this thought is now abandoned. Children in the earlier grades may properly spend more time in object study than in later grades, but there is no time in school life when we can afford to cut loose from the real world. There is scarcely a lesson in any subject that can not be clarified and strengthened by calling in the fresh experiences of daily life.

The discussion of the concept and of the inductive process has shown that *concepts cannot be found at first hand*. There must be observation of different objects, comparison, and grouping into a class. A person who has never seen an elephant nor a picture of one, can form no adequate notion of elephants in general. We can by no shift dispense with the illustrations. The more the memory is filled with vivid pictures of real things, the more easy and rapid will be the progress to general truths. Not only are general notions of classes of objects in nature, or of personal actions built up out of particulars, but the general laws and principles of nature and of human society must be observed in real life to be understood. We should have no faith in *electricity* if it were simply a scientific theory, if it had not demonstrated its power through material objects. The idea of *cohesion* would never have been dreamed of, if it had not become necessary to explain certain physical facts. The spherical form of the earth was not accepted by many even learned men until sailors with ships had gone around it. Political ideas of popular government which a few centuries ago were regarded as purely utopian are now accepted as facts because they have become matters of common observation. The *circulation of the blood* remained a secret for many centuries because of the difficulties of bringing it home to the knowledge of the senses. These examples will show how difficult it is to go beyond the reach of sense experience. Even those philosophers who have tried to construct theories without the safe foundation of facts have labored for naught. The more our thought is checked and guided by nature's realities the less danger of inflation with pretended knowledge. Bacon found that in this tendency to theorize loosely upon a slender basis of facts was the fundamental weakness of ancient philosophy. Nature if observed will reiterate her truths till they become convincing verities, while the study of words and books alone produces a *quasi-knowledge* which often mistakes the symbol for the thing.

Having this thought in mind, *Comenius*, more than two and a half centuries ago, said, "It is certain that there is nothing in the understanding which has not been previously in the senses, and consequently to exercise the senses carefully in discriminating the differences of natural objects is to lay the foundation of all wisdom, all eloquence, and of all good and prudent action. The right instruction of youth does not consist in cramming them with a mass of words, phrases, sentences, and opinions collected from authors. In this way the youth are taught, like Æsop's crow in the fable, to adorn themselves with strange feathers. Why should we not, instead of dead books, open the living book of nature? Not the shadows of things, but the things themselves, which make an impression upon the senses and imagination, are to be brought before the youth."

There has always been a strong tendency in the schools to teach *words, definitions, and rules* without a sufficient knowledge of the objects and experiences of life that put meaning into these abstractions. The result is that all the prominent educational reformers have pointedly condemned the practice of learning words, names, etc., without a knowledge of the things signified. The difference is like that between learning the names of a list of persons at a reception, and being present to enter into acquaintance and conversation with the guests. The oft-quoted dictum of Kant is a laconic summary of this argument. "General notions (concepts) without sense-percepts are empty." The general definition of composite flowers means little or nothing to a child; but after a familiar acquaintance with the sunflower, dandelion, thistle, etc., such a general statement has a clear meaning. Concepts without the content derived from objects are like a frame without a picture, or a cistern without water. The table is spread and the dishes placed, but no refreshments are supplied.

Having completed the discussion of *intuition*, including object lessons, that is, the preparatory step to the inductive process, we reach the second, *reflection* and *survey*. We are seeking for a general term that covers the several steps in the latter part of the inductive process. It includes comparison, classification, and abstraction. It may be discussed from the standpoint of "association of ideas," and contributes directly to concentration.

We have in mind, chiefly, that thoughtful habit which is not satisfied with simply acquiring a new fact or set of ideas, but is impelled to trace them out along their various connections. We have to do now not with the acquisition but with the *elaboration* and *assimilation* of knowledge. The *acquisition* of knowledge in the ordinary sense is one thing; its *elaboration* in a full sense sets up a standard of progress which will put life into all school work and reach far beyond it, and in fact is limited only by the individual capacity for thought. In school, in reading and study, we have been largely engaged in acquiring knowledge on the principle that "knowledge is power." But no practical man needs to be told that much so-called school knowledge is not power. Facts which have been simply stored in the memory are often of little ready use. It is like wheat in the bin, which must first pass through the mill and change its entire form before it will perform its function. Facts, in order to become the personal property of the owner, must be worked over, sifted, sorted, classified, and connected. The process of elaborating and assimilating knowledge is so important that it requires more time and pains than the first labor of acquisition. Philosophers will admit this at once, but it is hard for us to break loose from the traditions of the schoolmasters. The mind is not in all respects like a *lumber-yard*. It is, to be sure, a place for storing up knowledge, just as the yard is a deposit for lumber. But there the analogy ceases and the mind begins to resemble more the contractor and builder. There is planing, sawing, and hammering; the materials collected are prepared, fitted, and mortised together, and a building fit for use begins to rise. Knowledge also is for use, and not primarily for storage. That simple acquisition and quantity of knowledge are not enough is illustrated by the analogy of an army. Numbers do not make an army, but a rabble. A general first enlists raw recruits, drills and trains them through a long period, and finally combines them into an effective army. Many of our ideas when first received are like disorderly raw recruits. They need to be disciplined into proper action and to ready obedience.

In connection with assimilation the analogy between the *stomach* and the mind is of still greater interest. The food received into the stomach is taken up by the organs of digestion, assimilated and converted into blood. The process, however, takes its course without our conscious effort or co-operation. Knowledge likewise enters the mind, but how far will assimilation go on without conscious effort? If kept in a healthy state the organs of digestion are self active. Not so the mind. Ideas entering the mind are not so easily assimilated as the food materials that enter the stomach. A cow chews her cud once, but the ideas that enter our minds may be drawn from their receptacle in the memory and worked over again and again. Ideas have to be put side by side, separated, grouped, and arranged into connected series. There is, no doubt, some tendency in the mind toward involuntary assimilation, but it greatly needs culture and training. Many people never reach the *thinking* stage, never learn to survey and reflect. The tendency of the mind to work over and digest knowledge should receive ample culture in the schools. There is a mental inertia produced by pure memory exercise that is unfavorable to reflection. It requires an extra exertion to arrange and organize facts even after they are acquired. But when the habit of reflection has been inaugurated it adds much interest and value to all mental acquisitions.

There are also well-established principles which guide the mind in elaborating its facts. The *laws of the association* of ideas indicate clearly the natural trend of mental elaboration. The association of things because of contiguity in time and place is the simplest mode. The classification of objects or activities on the basis of resemblance, is the second form and that upon which the inductive process is principally founded. In the third case objects and series are easily retained in memory when the relation of cause and effect is perceived between them. These natural highways of association, especially the second and third, should be frequently traveled in linking the facts of school study with each other. Indeed the outcome of a rational survey of an object or fact in its different relations is an association of ideas which is one of the best results of study. Such connections of resemblance and difference or of cause and effect are abundant and interesting in the natural sciences and physical geography, also in history and languages.

The Herbartians draw an important distinction between *psychical* and *logical* concepts or general notions. The *psychical* concept is worked out naturally by a child or an adult as a result of the chance experiences of life. It is usually a work of accident; is incomplete, faulty, and often misleading. The *logical* concept, on the other hand, is scientifically correct and complete. It includes all the common characteristics of the group and excludes all that are not essential. It is a product of accurate and mature thinking. We all possess an abundance of psychical concepts drawn from the miscellaneous experiences of life. It is a large share of the school work, as we have seen, to develop logical concepts out of these immature and faulty psychical concepts. A child is disposed to call tadpoles fishes; and later porpoises and whales are faultily classed with the fishes in the same way. Nearly all our psychical concepts are subject to such loose and faulty judgments. Even where one is accurate in his observations, the conclusions naturally drawn are often wrong. For example, a child that has seen none but red squirrels would naturally think all squirrels red, and include the quality red in his general notion. Most of our empirically derived general notions are spotted with such defects. What relation have these facts to induction? We claim that general notions should be experimentally formed; that is, by a gradual collection of concrete or illustrative materials, and that the logical concepts are the final outcome of comparison and reasoning toward conclusions. In other words, we must begin with psychical concepts with all their faults; we must make mistakes and correct them as our experience enlarges, and gradually work out of psychical into logical methods and results. Our text-books usually give us the logical concept first, the rule, definition, principle, in its most complete and accurate statement. This does violence to the child's natural mental movement.

The final stage of induction is the *formulation* of the general truths, the concepts, principles, and laws which constitute the science of any branch of knowledge. These truths should be well formulated in clear and expressive language and mastered in this form. Moreover, the results reached, when reduced to the strict scientific form, are the same in the inductive methods as in the deductive or common text-book method. Not that the effect on the mind of the learner is the same but the body of truth is unaltered. The general truths of every subject can be easily found well arranged in text-books. But we are more anxious to know how the youth may best approach and appreciate these truths than simply to see them stored in the mind in a well-classified form.

A rich man in leaving a fortune to his son would more than double the value of the inheritance if he could teach him properly to *appreciate* wealth and form in him the disposition and ability to use it wisely. In the same way the best part of knowledge is not simply its possession, but an appreciation of its value. The method of reaching scientific knowledge through the inductive process, that is by the collection and comparison of data with a view to positive insight, will give greater meaning to the results. Interest is awakened and self-activity exercised at every step in the progress toward general truths. By the reflective habit these truths will be seen in their origin and causal connection, and the line of similarity, contrast, causal relation, analogy and coincidence will be thoughtfully traced.

Possibly the progress toward formulated knowledge will be less rapid by induction, but it will be real progress with no backward steps. It may well be doubted whether, with average minds, real scientific knowledge is attainable except by a strong admixture of inductive processes. Perfection in the form and structure of our concepts is not to be attained by children nor by adults, but the ideal of scientific accuracy in general notions is to be kept constantly in view and approximated to the extent of our ability.

After all, *deduction* performs a much more important part in the work of building up concepts than the previous discussion would indicate. As fast as psychical concepts are formed we clamber upon them and try to get a better view of the field around us. Like captured guns, we turn them at once upon the enemy and make them perform service in new fields of conquest. If a new case or object appears we judge of it in the light of our acquired concepts, no matter whether they are complete and accurate or not. This is deduction. We are glad to gain any vantage ground in judging the objects and phenomena constantly presenting themselves. In fact, it is inevitable that inductive and deductive processes will be constantly dovetailed into each other. The faulty concepts arrived at are brought persistently into contact with new individual cases. They are thus corrected, enlarged, and more accurately grasped. This is the series of mental stepping-stones that leads up gradually to logical concepts. The inductive process is the fundamental one and deduction comes in at every step to brace it up. This is only another illustration that mental processes are intimately interwoven, and, except in thought, not to be separated. In the discussion of apperception in the following chapter we shall see that, in the process of gaining knowledge, our acquired ideas and concepts play a most important role. They are really the chief assimilating agencies. But in spite of all this we shall scarcely be led again to the standpoint that logical or scientific concepts should be the starting point in the study of any subject.

CHAPTER VI.

APPERCEPTION.

We have now to deal with a principle of pedagogy upon which all the leading ideas thus far discussed largely depend for their realization. Interest, concentration, and induction set up requirements relative to the matter, spirit, and method of school studies. Apperception is a practical principle, obedience to which will contribute daily and hourly to making real in school exercises the ideas of interest, concentration and induction.

We observe in passing that the important principles already discussed stand in close mutual relation and dependence. Interest aids concentration by bringing all kinds of knowledge into close touch with the feelings. Interest puts incentives into every kind of information so as to arouse the will, which, in turn, unifies and controls the mental actions. But concentration has a reflex influence upon interest, because unity and conscious mastery give added pleasure to knowledge. The culture epochs are expected to contribute powerfully to both concentration and interest; to the former by supplying a series of rallying-points for educative effort, to the latter by furnishing matter suited to interest children. Induction is a natural method of acquiring and unifying knowledge in an interesting way. Apperception, in turn, is a principle of mental action which puts life and interest into inductive and concentrating processes. Every hour of school labor illustrates the value of apperception and teachers should find in it a constant antidote to faulty methods.

Apperception may be roughly defined at first as the process of *acquiring new ideas by the aid of old ideas* already in the mind. It makes the acquisition of new knowledge easier and quicker. Not that there is any easy road to learning, but there is a natural process which greatly accelerates the progress of acquisition, just as it is better to follow a highway over a rough country than to betake one's self to the stumps and brush. For example, if one is familiar with peaches, apricots will be quickly understood as a kindred kind of fruit, even though a little strange. A person who is familiar with electrical machinery will easily interpret the meaning and purpose of every part of a new electrical plant. One may *perceive* a new object without understanding it, but to *apperceive* it is to interpret its meaning by the aid of similar familiar notions.

If one examines a *typewriter* for the first time, it will take some pains and effort to understand its construction and use; but after examining a Remington, another kind will be more easily understood, because the principle of the first interprets that of the second. Suppose the *Steppes of Russia* are mentioned for the first time to a class. The word has little or no meaning or perhaps suggests erroneously a succession of stairs. But we remark that the steppes are like the prairies and plains to the west of the Mississippi river, covered with grass and fed on by herds. By awakening a familiar notion already in the mind and bringing it distinctly to the front, the new thing is easily understood. Again, a boy goes to town and sees a *banana* for the first time, and asks, "What is that? I never saw anything like that." He thinks he has no class of things to which it belongs, no place to put it. His father answers that it is to eat like an orange or a pear, and its significance is at once plain by the reference to something familiar.

Again, two men, the one a *machinist* and the other an observer unskilled in machines, visit the machinery hall of an exposition. The machinist observes a new invention and finds in it a new application of an old principle. As he passes along from one machine to another he is much interested in noting new devices and novel appliances and at the end of an hour he leaves the hall with a mind enriched. The other observer sees the same machines and their parts, but does not detect the principle of their construction. His previous knowledge of machines is not sufficient to give him the clue to their explanation. After an hour of uninterested observation he leaves the hall with a confused notion of shafts, wheels, cogs, bands, etc., but with no greater insight into the principles of machinery. Why has one man learned so much and the other nothing? Because the machinist's previous experience served as an interpreter and explained these new contrivances, while the other had no sufficient previous knowledge and so acquired nothing new. "To him that hath shall be given."

In the act of apperception the old ideas dwelling in the mind are not to be regarded as dead treasures stored away and only occasionally drawn out and used by a purposed effort of the memory, but they are *living forces* which have the active power of seizing and appropriating new ideas. Lazarus says they stand "like well-armed men in the inner stronghold of the mind ready to sally forth and overcome or make serviceable whatever shows itself at the portals of sense." It is then through the active aid of familiar ideas that new things find an introduction to soul life. If old friends go out to meet the strangers and welcome them, there will be an easy entrance and a quick adoption into the new home.

But frequently these old friends who stand in the background of our thoughts must be *awakened* and called to the front. They must stand as it were on tiptoe ready to welcome the stranger. For if they lie asleep in the penetralia of the home the new comers may approach and pass by for lack of a welcome. It is often necessary, therefore, for the teacher to revive old impressions, to call up previously acquired knowledge and to put it in readiness to receive and welcome the new. The success with which this is done is often the difference between good and poor teaching.

We might suppose that when two persons look at the same object they would get the *same impression*, but this is not true at all. Where one person faints with fright or emotion another sees nothing to be disturbed at. Two travelers come in sight of an old homestead. To one it is an object of absorbing interest as the home of his childhood; to the other it is much like any other old farm house. What is the cause of this difference? Not the house. It is the same in both cases. It is remarkable how much color is given to every idea that enters into the mind by the ideas already there. Some visitors at the World's Fair can tell almost at a glance to what states many of the buildings belong; other visitors must study this out on the maps and notices. One who is familiar with the history, architecture, and products of the different states is able to classify many of the buildings with ease. His previous knowledge of these states interprets their buildings. Mt. Vernon naturally belongs to Virginia, Independence Hall to Pennsylvania, John Hancock's house to Massachusetts. In a still more striking manner, a knowledge of foreign countries enables the observer to classify such buildings as the French, the German, the Swedish, the Japanese, etc. Again, in viewing any exhibit our enjoyment and appreciation depend almost entirely upon our previous knowledge, not upon our eye-sight or our physical endurance. Many objects of the greatest value we pass by with an indifferent glance because our previous knowledge is not sufficient to give us their meaning.

If a dry goods merchant, a horse jockey, and an architect pass down a city street together, what will each observe? The merchant notices all the dry goods stores, their displays, and their favorable or unfavorable location. The jockey sees every horse and equipage; he forms a quiet but quick judgment upon every passing animal. The architect sees the buildings and style of construction. If in the evening each is called upon to give his observations for the day, the jockey talks of horses and describes some of the best specimens in detail; the merchant speaks of store-fronts and merchandise; the architect is full of elevations of striking or curious buildings. The architect and merchant remember nothing, perhaps, about the horses; the jockey nothing of stores or buildings. Three people may occupy the same pew in a church; the one can tell you all about the music, the second the good points in the sermon, and the third the style and becomingness of the bonnets and dresses. Each one sees what he has in his own mind. A teacher describes Yosemite Valley to a geography class. Some of the children construct a mental picture of a gorge with steep mountain sides, but no two pictures are alike; some have mental pictures that resemble nothing in heaven above or earth below; some have constructed— —nothing at all! only the echo of a few spoken words. If the teacher, at the close of her description, could have the mental state of each child photographed on the blackboard of her schoolroom she would be in mental distress. In presenting such topics to children, much depends upon the previous content of their minds, upon the colors out of which they paint the pictures.

We are now prepared for a more accurate *definition* of apperception. "The transformation of a newer (weaker) concept by means of an older one surpassing the former in power and inner organization bears the name of apperception, in contrast to the unaltered reception of the same perception." (Lindner's Psychol. p. 124, trans. by De Garmo.) Lindner remarks further, "Apperception is the reaction of the old against the new—in it is revealed the preponderance which the older, firmer, and more self-contained concept groups have in contrast to the concepts which have just entered consciousness." Again, "It is *a kind of process of condensation of thought* and brings into the mental life a certain stability and firmness, in that it subordinates new to older impressions, puts everything in its right place and in its right relation to the whole, and in this way works at that organic formation of our consciousness which we call *culture*." (Lindner p. 126.) "Apperception may be defined as that interaction between two similar ideas or thought-complexes in the course of which the weaker, unorganized, isolated idea or thought-complex is incorporated into the richer, better digested, and more firmly compacted one." (Lange, Apperception, p. 13.)

Oftentimes, therefore, older ideas or thought masses, being clear, strong, and well-digested receive a new impression to modify and appropriate it. This is especially true where opinions have been carefully formed after thought and deliberation. A well-trained political economist, for example, when approaching a new theory or presentation of it by a George or Bellamy, meets it with all the resources of a well-stored, thoughtful mind; and admits it, if at all, in a modified form to his system of thought. Sometimes, however, a new theory, which strikes the mind with great clearness and vigor, is able to make a powerful assault upon previous opinions, and perhaps modify or overturn them. This is the more apt to be the case if one's previous ideas have been weak and undecided. In the interaction between the old and new the latter then become the apperceiving forces. Upon the untrained or poorly-equipped mind a strong argument has a more decisive effect than it may justly deserve. As we noticed above, new ideas, especially those coming directly through the senses, are often more vivid and attractive than similar old ones. For this reason they usually occupy greater attention and prominence at first than later, when the old ideas have begun to revive and reassert themselves. Old ideas usually have the advantage over the new in being better organized, more closely connected in series and groups; and having been often repeated, they acquire a certain permanent ascendency in the thoughts. In this interaction between similar notions, old and new, the differences at first arrest attention, then gradually sink into the background, while the stronger points of resemblance begin to monopolize the thought and bind the notions into a unity.

The use of familiar notions in acquiring an insight into new things is a *natural tendency* or drift of the mind. As soon as we see something new and desire to understand it, at once we involuntarily begin to ransack our old stock of ideas to discover anything in our previous experience which corresponds to this or is like it. For whatever is like it or has an analogy to it, or serves the same uses, will explain this new thing, though the two objects be in other points essentially different. We are, in short, constantly falling back upon our old experiences and classifications for the explanation of new objects that appear to us.

So far is this true that the *most ordinary things* can only be explained in the light of experience. When John Smith wrote a note to his companions at Jamestown, and thus communicated his desires to them, it was unintelligible to the Indians. They had no knowledge of writing and looked on the marks as magical. When *Columbus' ships* first appeared on the cost of the new world, the natives looked upon them as great birds. They had never seen large sailing vessels. To vary the illustration, the *art of reading*, so easy to a student, is the accumulated result of a long collection of knowledge and experience. There is an unconscious employment of apperception in the practical affairs of life that is of interest. We often see a person at a distance and by some slight characteristic of motion, form, or dress, recognize him at once. From this slight trace we picture to ourselves the person in full and say we saw him in the street. Sitting in my room at evening I hear the regular passenger train come in. The noise alone suggests the engine, cars, conductor, passengers, and all the train complete. As a matter of fact I saw nothing at all but have before my mind the whole picture. On Sunday morning I see some one enter a familiar church door, and going on my way the whole picture of church, congregation, pastor, music and sermon come distinctly to my mind. Only a passing glance at one person entering suggests the whole scene. In looking at a varied landscape we see many things which the sensuous eye alone would not detect, distances, perspective and relative size, position and nature of objects. This apperceptive power is of vast importance in practical life as it leads to quick judgment and action, when personal examinations into details would be impossible.

In apperception we never pass from the known to things which are *entirely new*. Absolutely new knowledge is gained by perception or intuition. When an older person meets with something totally new, he either does not notice it or it staggers him. Apperception does not take place. In many cases we are disturbed or frightened, as children, by some new or sudden noise or object. But most so-called new things bear sufficient resemblance to things seen before to admit of explanation. Strange as the sights of a Chinese city might appear, we should still know that we were in a city. In most "new" objects of observation or study, the familiar parts greatly preponderate over the unfamiliar. In a new reading lesson, for example, most of the words and ideas are well known, only an occasional word requires explanation and that by using familiar illustrations. The flood of our familiar and oft-repeated ideas sweeps on like a great river, receiving here and there from either side a tributary stream, that is swallowed up in its waters without perceptible increase.

So strong is the apperceiving force of familiar notions that they drag far-distant scenes in geography and history into the home neighborhood and locate them there. The *imagination* works in conjunction with the apperceiving faculty and constructs real pictures. Children are otherwise inclined to substitute one thing for another by imagination. With boys and girls, geographical objects about home are often converted by fancy into representatives of distant places. It is related of *Byron* that while reading in childhood the story of the Trojan war, he localized all the places in the region of his home. An old hill and castle looking toward the plain and the sea were his Troy. The stream flowing through the plain was the Simois. The places of famous conflicts between the Trojans and Greeks were located. So vivid were the pictures which these home scenes gave to the child, that years later in visiting Asia Minor and the sight of the real Troy, he was not so deeply impressed as in his boyhood. A *German professor* relates that he and his companions, while reading the Indian stories of Cooper, located the important scenes in the hills and valleys about Eisenach in the Thuringian mountains. Many other illustrations of the same imaginative tendency to substitute home objects for foreign ones are given. But whether or not this experience is true of us all, it is certain that we can form no idea of foreign places and events except as we *construct* the pictures out of the *fragments* of things that we have known. What we have seen of rivers, lands, and cities must form the materials for picturing to ourselves distant places.

Since the old ideas have so much to do with the proper reception of the new, let us examine more closely the *interaction* of the two. If a *new idea* drops into the mind, like a stone upon the surface of the water, it produces a commotion. It acts as a stimulus or wakener to the old ideas sleeping beneath the surface. It draws them up above the surface-level; that is, into consciousness. But what ideas are thus disturbed? There are thousands of these latent ideas, embryonic thoughts, beneath the surface. Those which possess sufficient kinship to this new-comer to hear his call, respond. For in the mind "birds of a feather flock together." Ideas and thoughts which resemble the new one answer, the others sleep on undisturbed, except a few who are so intimately associated with these kinsmen as to be disturbed when they are disturbed. Or, to state it differently, certain thought-groups or complexes, which contain elements kindred to the new notion, are agitated and raised into conscious thought. They seem to respond to their names. The new idea may continue for some time to stimulate and agitate. There appears to be a sort of telegraphic inquiry through the regions of the mind to find out where the kindred dwell. The distant relatives and strangers (the unrelated or unserviceable ideas) soon discover that they have responded to the wrong call and drop back to sleep again. But the real kindred wake up more and more. They come forward to inspect the new-comer and to examine his credentials. Soon he finds that he is surrounded by inquisitive friends and relatives. They threaten even to take possession of him. Up to this point the new idea has taken the lead, he has been the aggressor. But now is the time for the awakened kindred ideas to assume control and lead the stranger captive, to bring him in among themselves and give him his appropriate place and importance. The *old body of ideas*, when once set in motion, is more powerful than any single-handed stranger who happens to fall into their company. The outcome is that the stranger, who at first seemed to be producing such a sensation, now discovers that strong arms are about him and he is carried captive by vigorous friends. New ideas when first entering the mind are very strong, and, if they come through the senses, are especially rich in the color and vigor of real life. They therefore absorb the attention at first and seem to monopolize the mental energies; but the older thought masses, when fully aroused, are better organized, more firmly rooted in habit, and possess much wider connections. They are almost certain, therefore, to apperceive the new idea; that is, to conquer and subdue it, to make it tributary to their power.

Let us examine more closely the *effect* of the process of apperception upon the new and old ideas that are brought in contact. First, observe the effect upon the *new*: Many an idea which is not strong enough in itself to make a lasting impression, upon the mind would quickly fade out and be forgotten were it not that in this process the old ideas throw it into a clear light, give it more meaning, associate it closely with themselves, and thus save it. Two persons look at the sword of Washington; one examines it with deep interest, the other scarcely gives it a second glance. The one remembers it for life, the other forgets it in an hour. The sense perception was the same in both persons at first, but the reception given to the idea by one converts it into a lasting treasure. A little lamp-black, rolled up between finger and thumb, suggested to Edison his carbon points for the electric light. A piece of lamp-black would produce no such effect in most peoples minds. The difference is in the reception accorded to an idea. The meaning and importance of an idea or event depend upon the interpretation put upon it by our previous experience. "Many a weak, obscure, and fleeting perception would pass almost unnoticed into obscurity, did not the additional activity of apperception hold it fast in consciousness. This sharpens the senses, *i.e.*, it gives to the organs of sense a greater degree of energy, so that the watching eye now sees, and the listening ear now hears, that which ordinarily would pass unnoticed. The events of apperception give to the senses a peculiar keenness, which underlies the skill of the money-changer in detecting a counterfeit among a thousand bank-notes, notwithstanding its deceptive similarity; of the jeweler who marks the slightest, apparently imperceptible, flaw in an ornament; of the physicist who perceives distinctly the overtones of a vibrating string. According to this we see and hear not only with the eye and ear, but quite as much with the help of our present knowledge, with the apperceiving content of the mind." (Apperception, Lange, De Garmo, p. 21.)

Some even intelligent and sensible people can walk through Westminster Abbey and see nothing but a curious old church with a few graves and monuments. To a person well-versed in English history and literature it is a shrine of poets, a temple of heroes, the common resting-place of statesmen and kings.

Secondly, what is the *effect on the old ideas*? Every idea that newly enters the mind produces changes in the older groups and series of thought. Any one new idea may cause but slight changes, but the constant influx of new experiences works steadily at a modification and rearrangement of our previous stores of thought. Faulty and incomplete groups and concepts are corrected or enlarged; that is, changed from psychical into logical notions. Children are surprised to find little flowers on the oaks, maples, walnuts, and other large forest trees. On account of the small size of the blossoms, heretofore unnoticed, they had not thought of the great trees as belonging to the flowering plants. Their notion of flowering plants is, therefore, greatly enlarged by a few new observations. The bats flying about in the twilight have been regarded as birds; but a closer inspection shows that they belong to another class, and the notion bird must be limited. As already observed in the discussion of induction, most of our psychical notions are thus faulty and incomplete; *e.g.*, the ideas fruit, fish, star, insect, mineral, ship, church, clock, dog, kitchen, library, lawyer, city, etc. Our notions of these and of hundreds of other such classes are at first both incomplete and faulty. The inflow of new ideas constantly modifies them, extending, limiting, explaining, and correcting our previous concepts.

Sometimes, however, a single new thought may have wide-reaching effects; it may even revolutionize one's previous modes of thinking and reorganize one's activities about a new center. With Luther, for instance, the idea of justification by faith was such a new and potent force, breaking up and rearranging his old forms of thought. St. Paul's vision on the way to Damascus is a still more striking illustration of the power of a new idea or conviction. And yet, even in such cases, the old ideas reassert themselves with great persistence and power. Luther and St. Paul remained, even after these great changes, in many respects the same kind of men as before. Their old habits of thinking were modified, not destroyed; the direction of their lives was changed, but many of their habits and characteristics remained almost unaltered.

Apperception, however, is not limited to the effects of *external objects* upon us, to the influence of ideas coming from without upon our old stores of knowledge. Old ideas, long since stored in the mind, may be freshly called up and brought into such contact with each other that new results follow, new apperceptions take place. In moments of reflection we are often surprised by conclusions that had not presented themselves to us before. A new light dawns upon us and we are surprised at not having seen it before. In fact, it makes little difference whether the idea suggested to the mind comes from within or from without if, when it once enters fairly into consciousness, it has power to stimulate other thoughts, to wake up whole thought complexes and bring about a process of action and reaction between itself and others. The result is new associations, new conclusions, new mental products—apperceptions.

This *inner apperception*, as it has been sometimes called, takes place constantly when we are occupied with our own thoughts, rather than with external impressions. With persons of deep, steady, reflective habits, it is the chief means of organizing their mental stores. The feelings and the will have much also to do with this process.

The laws of association draw the *feelings* as much as the intellectual states into apperceptive acts. I hear of a friend who has had disasters in business and has lost his whole fortune. If I have never experienced such difficulties myself, the chances are that the news will not make a deep impression upon me. But if I have once gone through the despondency of such a crushing defeat, sympathy for my friend will be awakened, and I may feel his trouble almost as my own. The meaning of such an item of news depends upon the response which it finds in my own feelings. It is well known that those friends can best sympathize with us in our trouble who have passed through the same troubles. Even enemies are not lacking in sympathy with each other when an appeal is made to deep feelings and experiences common to both.

The feeling of *interest*, which we have emphasized so much, is chiefly, if not wholly, dependent upon apperceptive conditions. Select a lesson adapted to the age and understanding of a child, present it in such a way as to recall and make use of his previous experience, and interest is certain to follow. The outcome of a successful act of apperception is always a feeling of pleasure, or at least of interest. When the principle of apperception is fully applied in teaching, the progress from one point to another is so gradual and clear that it gives pleasure. The clearness and understanding with which we receive knowledge adds greatly to our interest in it. On the contrary, when apperception is violated, and new knowledge is only half understood and assimilated there can be but little feeling of satisfaction. "The overcoming of certain difficulties, the accession of numerous ideas, the success of the act of knowledge or recognition, the greater clearness that the ideas have gained, awaken a feeling of pleasure. We become conscious of the growth of our knowledge and power of understanding. The significance of this new impression for our ego is now more strongly felt than at the beginning or during the course of the progress. To this pleasurable feeling is easily added the effort, at favorable opportunity, to reproduce the product of the apperception, to supplement and deepen it, to unite it to other ideas, and so further to extend certain chains of thought. The summit or sum of these states of mind we happily express with the word interest. For in reality the feeling of self appears between the various stages of the process of apperception (*inter esse*); with one's whole soul does one contemplate the object of attention. If we regard the acquired knowledge as the objective result of apperception, interest must be regarded as the subjective side." (Lange, Apperception, page 19.)

Finally, the *will* has much to do with conscious efforts at apperception. It holds the thought to certain groups; it excludes or pushes back irrelevant ideas that crowd in; it holds to a steady comparison of ideas, even where perplexity and obscurity trouble the thinker. When the process of reaching a conclusion takes much time, when conflict or contradiction have to be removed or adjusted, when reflection and reasoning are necessary, the will is of great importance in giving coherency and steadiness to the apperceptive effort. A conscious effort at apperception, therefore, may include many elements, sense perceptions, ideas recalled, feeling, *will*.

"Let us now sum up the essentials in the process of apperception. First of all, an external or internal perception, an idea, or idea-complex appears in consciousness, finding more or less response in the mind; that is, giving rise to greater or less stimulation to thought and feeling.

"In consequence of this, and in accordance with the psychical mechanism or an impulse of the will, one or more groups of thoughts arise, which enter into relation to the perception. While the two masses are compared with one another, they work upon one another with more or less of a transforming power. New thought-combinations are formed, until, finally, the perception is adjusted to the stronger and older thought combination. In this way all the factors concerned gain in value as to knowledge and feeling; especially, however, does the new idea gain a clearness and activity that it never would have gained for itself. *Apperception is, therefore, that psychical activity by which individual perceptions, ideas, or idea-complexes are brought into relation to our previous intellectual and emotional life, assimilated with it, and thus raised to greater clearness, activity, and significance.*" (Lange, Apperception, page 41.)

Important *conclusions* drawn from a study of apperception:

1. *Value of previous knowledge.* If knowledge once acquired is so *valuable* we are first of all urged to make the acquisition permanent. Thorough mastery and frequent reviews are necessary to make knowledge stick. Careless and superficial study is injurious. It is sometimes carelessly remarked by those who are supposed to be wise in educational matters that it makes no difference how much we forget

if we only have proper drill and training to study. That is, how we study is more important than what we learn. But viewed in the light of apperception, acquired knowledge should be retained and used, for it unlocks the door to more knowledge. *Thorough mastery and retention* of the elements of knowledge in the different branches is the only solid road to progress. In this connection we can see the importance of learning only what is *worth remembering*, what will prove a valuable treasure in future study. In the selection of material for school studies, therefore, we must keep in mind knowledge which, as Comenius says, is of *solid utility*. Having once selected and acquired such materials, we are next impelled to make *constant use* of them. If the acquisition of new information depends so much upon the right use of previous knowledge, we are called upon to build constantly upon this foundation. This is true whether the child's knowledge has been acquired at school or at home. In order to make things clear and interesting to boys and girls we must refer every day to what they have before learned in school and out of school.

Again, if we accept the doctrine that old ideas are the materials out of which we constantly build *bridges* across into new fields of knowledge, we must *know the children* better and what store of knowledge they have already acquired. Just as an army marching into a new country must know well the country through which it has passed and must keep open the line of communication and the base of supplies, so the student must always have a safe retreat into his past, and a base of supplies to sustain him in his onward movements. The tendency is very strong for a grade teacher to think that she needs to know nothing except the facts to be acquired in her own grade. But she should remember that her grade is only a station on the highway to learning and life. In teaching we cannot by any shift dispense with the ideas children have gained at home, at play, in the school and outside of it. This, in connection with what the child has learned in the previous grades, constitutes a stock of ideas, a capital, upon which the teacher should freely draw in illustrating daily lessons.

2. The use of our acquired stock of ideas involves a constant *working over* of old ideas, and this working-over process not only reviews and strengthens past knowledge, keeping it from forgetfulness, but it throws new light upon it and exposes it to a many-sided criticism. In the first place familiar ideas should not be allowed to rest in the mind *unused*. Like tools for service they must be kept bright and sharp. One reason why so many of the valuable ideas we have acquired have gradually disappeared from the mind is because they remained so long unused that they faded out of sight. The old saying that "repetition is the mother of studies" needs to be recalled and emphasized. By being put in contact, with new ideas, old notions are seen and appreciated in new relations. Facts that have long lain unexplained in the mind, suddenly receive a *new interpretation*, a vivid and rational meaning. Or the old meaning is intensified and vivified by putting a new fact in conjunction with it.

Where the climate and products of the British Isles have been studied in political geography, and later on, in physical geography, the gulf stream is explained in its bearings on the climate of western Europe, the whole subject of the climate of England is viewed from a new and interesting standpoint. In arithmetic, where the sum of the squares of the two sides of a right-angled triangle is illustrated by an example and later on in geometry the same proposition is taken up in a different way and proved as a universal theorem, new and interesting light is thrown upon an old problem of arithmetic. In *United States history*, after the Revolution has been studied, the biography of a man like Samuel Adams throws much additional and vivid light upon the events and actors in Boston and Massachusetts. The life of John Adams would give a still different view of the same great events; just as a city, as seen from different standpoints, presents different aspects.

3. We have thus far shown that new ideas are more easily understood and assimilated when they are brought into close contact with what we already know; and secondly, that our old knowledge is often explained and illuminated by new facts brought to bear upon it. We may now observe the result of this double action—*the welding* of old and new into one piece, the close mingling and association of all our knowledge, *i.e.*, its unity. Apperception, therefore, has the same final tendency that was observed in the *inductive process*, the unification of knowledge, the concentration of all experience by uniting its parts into groups and series. The smith, in welding together two pieces of iron, heats both and then hammers them together into one piece. The teacher has something similar to do. He must revive old ideas in the child's mind, then present the new facts and bring the two things together while they are still fresh, so as to cause them to coalesce. To prove this observe how long division may be best taught. Call up and review the method of short division, then proceed to work a problem in long division calling attention to the similar steps and processes in the two, and finally to the difference between them.

The defect of much teaching in children's classes is that the *teacher* does not properly provide for the welding together of the new and old. The important practical question after all is whether instructors see to it that children recall their previous knowledge. It is necessary to take special pains in this. Nothing is more common than to find children forgetting the very thing which, if remembered, would explain the difficult point in the lesson. Teachers are often surprised that children have forgotten things once learned. But, in an important sense, we encourage children to forget by not calling into use their acquisitions. Lessons are learned too much, each by itself, without reference to what precedes or what follows, or what effect this lesson of to-day may have upon things learned a year ago. Putting it briefly, children and teachers do not *think* enough, pondering things over in their minds, relating facts with each other, and bringing all knowledge into unity, and into a clear comprehension. The habit of *thoughtfulness*, engendered by a proper combining of old and new, is one of the valuable results of a good education. It gives the mind a disposition to glance backward or forward, to judge of all old ideas from a broader, more intelligent standpoint. Thinking everything over in the light of the best experience we can bring to bear upon it, prevents us from jumping at conclusions.

The general *plan of all studies* is based upon this notion of acquiring knowledge by the assistance of accumulated funds. In *Arithmetic* it would be folly to begin with long division before the multiplication table is learned. In *Geometry*, later propositions depend upon earlier principles and demonstrations. In *Latin*, vocabularies and inflections and syntactical relations must be mastered before readiness in the use of language is reached. And so it is to a large degree in the general plan of all studies. In spite of this no principle is more commonly violated in daily recitations than that of apperception. Its value is self-evident as a principle for the arrangement of topics in any branch of study, but it is overlooked in daily lessons. Instead of this new knowledge is acquired by a thoughtless memory drill.

In this welding process we desire to determine how far an actual concentration may take place *between school studies* and *the home and outside life of children*. The stock of ideas and feelings which a child from its infancy has gathered from its peculiar history and home surroundings is the primitive basis of its personality. Its thought, feeling, and individuality are deeply interwoven with home experience. No other set of ideas, later acquired, lies so close to its heart or is so abiding in its memory. The memory of work and play at home; of the house, yard, trees, and garden; of parents, brothers, and sisters, and in addition to this the experiences connected with neighbors and friends, the town and surrounding country, the church and its influence, the holidays, games, and celebrations, all these things lie deeper in the minds of children than the facts learned about grammar, geography, or history in school. Any plan of education that ignores these home-bred ideas, these events, memories, and sympathies of home and neighborhood life, will make a vital mistake. A concentration that keeps in mind only the school studies and disregards the rich funds of ideas that every child brings from his home, must be a failure, because it only includes the weaker half of his experience. Home knowledge itself does not need to be made a concentrating center, but all its best materials must be drawn into the concentrating center of the school. But children bring many faulty, mistaken, and even vicious ideas from their homes. It is well to know the actual situation. It is the work of the school, at every step, while receiving, to correct, enlarge, or arrange the faulty or disordered knowledge brought into the school by children. We unconsciously use these materials, and depend upon them for explaining new lessons, more constantly than we are aware of. In fact, if we were wise teachers, we would consciously make a more frequent use of them and, in order to render them more valuable, take special pains to review, correct, and arrange them. We would teach children to observe more closely and to remember better the things they daily see.

We shall appreciate better the value of *home knowledge* if we take note of the direct and constant dependence of the most important studies upon it. We usually think of history as something far away in New England, or France, or Egypt. History is mainly the study of the actions, customs, homes, and institutions of men in different countries. But what an abundance of similar facts and observations a child has gathered about home before he begins the study of history. From his infancy he has seen people of all sorts and conditions, rich and poor, ignorant and learned, honorable and mean. He has seen all sorts of human actions, learned to know their meaning and to pass judgment upon them. He has seen houses, churches, public buildings, trade and commerce, and a hundred human institutions. The child has been studying human actions and institutions in the concrete for a dozen years before he begins to read and recite history from books. Without the knowledge thus acquired out of school, society, government, and institutions would be worse than Greek. Geography as taught in the books would be totally foreign and strange but for the abundance of ideas the child has already picked up about hills, streams, roads, travel, storms, trees, animals, and people.

Natural science lessons must be based on a more careful study of things already seen about home—rocks and streams, flowers and plants, animals wild and tame. These with the forests, fields, brooks, seasons, tools, and inventions, are the necessary object lessons in natural science which can serve daily to illustrate other lessons. How near then do the natural science topics, geography and history, stand to the daily home life of a child! How intimate should be the relations which the school should establish between the parts of a child's experience! This is concentration in the broadest sense. A proper appreciation of this principle will save us from a number of common errors. Besides constantly associating home and school knowledge, we shall try to know the home and parents better, and the disposition and surroundings of each child. We shall be ready at any time to render home knowledge more clear and accurate, to correct faulty observation and opinion. While the children will be encouraged to illustrate lessons from their own experience, we shall fall into the excellent habit of explaining new and difficult points by a direct appeal to what the pupils have seen and understood. In short, there will be a disposition to draw into the concentrating work of the school all the deeper but outside life-experiences which form so important an element in the character of every person, which, however, teachers so often overlook. No other institution has such an opportunity or power to concentrate knowledge and experience as the school.

4. Another valuable educative result of apperception, cultivated in this manner, is a *consciousness of power* which springs from the ability to make a good use of our knowledge. The oftener children become aware that they have made a good use of acquired knowledge, the more they are encouraged. They see the treasure growing in their hands and feel conscious of their ability to use it. There is a mental exhilaration like that coming from abundant physical strength and health.

"Let us look back again at the results of our investigation. We observed first what essential services apperception performs for the human mind in the acquisition of new ideas, and for what an extraordinary easement and unburdening the acquiring soul is indebted to it. Should apperception once fail, or were it not implied in the very nature of our minds, we should, in the reception of sense-impressions, daily expend as much power as the child in its earliest years, since the perpetually changing objects of the external world would nearly always appear strange and new. We should gain the mastery of external things more slowly and painfully, and arrive much later at a certain conclusion of our external experience than we do now, and thereby remain perceptibly behind in our mental development. Like children with their A B C, we should be forced to take careful note of each word, and not, as now, allow ourselves actually to perceive only a few words in each sentence. In a word, without apperception our minds, with strikingly greater and more exhaustive labor, would attain relatively smaller results. Indeed, we are seldom conscious of the extent to which our perception is supported by apperception; of how it releases the senses from a large part of their labor, so that in reality we listen usually with half an ear or with a divided attention; nor, on the other hand, do we ordinarily reflect that apperception lends the sense organs a greater degree of energy, so that they perceive with greater sharpness and penetration than were otherwise possible. We do not consider that apperception spares us the trouble of examining ever anew and in small detail all the objects and phenomena that present themselves to us, so as to get their meaning, or that it thus prevents our mental power from scattering and from being worn out with wearisome, fruitless detail labors. The secret of its extraordinary success lies in the fact that it refers the new to the old, the strange to the familiar, the unknown to the known, that which is not comprehended to what is already understood and thus constitutes a part of our mental furniture; that it transforms the difficult and unaccustomed into the accustomed and causes us to grasp everything new by means of old-time, well-known ideas. Since, then, it accomplishes great and unusual results by small means, in so far as it reserves for the soul the greatest amount of power for other purposes, it agrees with the general principle of the least expenditure of force, or with that of the best adaptability of means to ends.

"As in the reception of new impressions, so also in working over and developing the previously acquired content of the mind, the helpful work of apperception shows itself. By connecting isolated things with mental groups already formed, and by assigning to the new its proper place among them, apperception not only increases the clearness and definiteness of ideas, but knits them more firmly to our consciousness. *Apperceiving ideas are the best aids to memory*. Again, so often as it subordinates new impressions to older ones, it labors at the association and articulation of the manifold materials of perception and thought. By condensing the content of observation and thinking into concepts and rules, or general experiences and principles, or ideals and general notions, apperception produces connection and order in our knowledge and volition. With its assistance there spring up those universal thought complexes, which, distributed to the various fields to which they belong, appear as logical, linguistic, aesthetic, moral, and religious norms or principles. If these acquire a higher degree of value for our feelings, if we find ourselves heartily attached to them, so that we prefer them to all those things which are contradictory, if we bind them to our own self, they will thus become powerful mental groups, which spring up independent of the psychical mechanism as often as kindred ideas appear in the mind. In the presence of these they now make manifest their apperceiving power. We measure and estimate them now according to universal laws. They are, so to speak, the eyes and hand of the will, with which, regulating and supplementing, rejecting and correcting, it lays a grasp upon the content as well as upon the succession of ideas. They hinder the purely mechanical flow of thought and desire, and our involuntary absorption in external impressions and in the varied play of fancy. We learn how to control religious impulses by laws, to rule thoughts by thoughts. In the place of the mechanical, appears the regulated course of thinking; in the place of the psychical rule of caprice, the monarchical control of higher laws and principles, and the spontaneity of the ego as the kernel of the personality. By the aid of apperception, therefore, we are lifted gradually from psychical bondage to mental and moral freedom. And now when ideal norms are apperceivingly active in the field of knowledge and thought, of feeling and will, when they give laws to the psychical mechanism, true culture is attained." (Lange's Apperception, edited by DeGarmo, p. 99, etc.)

> NOTE.—The freedom with which we quote extensively from Lange is an acknowledgement of the importance of his treatise. We are indebted to it throughout for many of the ideas treated.

CHAPTER VII.

THE WILL.

We have now completed the discussion of the concept-bearing or inductive process in learning and apperception, and find that they both tend to the unifying of knowledge and to the awakening of interest.

It remains to be seen how the will may be brought into activity and placed in command of the resources of the mind.

The *will* is that power of the mind which chooses, decides, and controls action.

According to psychology there are three distinct activities of the mind, *knowing, feeling,* and *willing*. These three powers are related to one another on a basis of equality, and yet the will should become the *monarch of the mind*. It is expected that all the other activities of the mind will be brought into subjection to the will. For strong *character* resides in the will. Strength of character depends entirely upon the mastery which the will has acquired over the life; and *the formation of character,* as shown in a strong moral will, is the highest aim of education.

The *great problem* for us to solve is: 1. How far can teaching stimulate and develop such a will?

There is an apparent contradiction in saying that the *will* is the monarch of the mind, the power which must control and subject all the other powers; and yet that it can be trained, educated, moulded, and chiefly too by a proper cultivation of the other powers, *feeling* and *knowing*. Knowledge and feeling, while they are subject to the will, still constitute its strength, just as the soldiers and officers of an army are subject to a commander and yet make him powerful.

We shall first notice the dependence of the will upon the *knowing* faculty. It is an old saying "that knowledge is power." But it is power only as a strong will is able to convert knowledge into action. Before the will can *decide* to do any given act it must see its way clearly. It must at least believe in the possibility. *In trying to get across a stream,* for example, if one can not swim and there is no bridge nor boat nor means of making one, the will can not act. It is helpless. The will must be shown the way to its aims or they are impossible. The more clear and distinct our knowledge, the better we can lay our plans and *will* to carry them out. It would be impossible for one of us *to will* to run a steam engine from Chicago to St. Paul to-day. We don't know how, and we should not be permitted to try. In every field of action we must have knowledge, and clear knowledge, before the will can act to good advantage. It is only knowledge, or at least faith in the possibility of accomplishing an undertaking, that opens the way to will. Much successful *experience* in any line of work brings increasing confidence and the will is greatly strengthened, because one knows that certain actions are possible. The simple acquisition of facts therefore, the increase of knowledge so long as it is well digested, makes it possible for the will to act with greater energy in various directions. The more clear this knowledge is, the more thoroughly it is cemented together in its parts and subject to control, the greater and more effective can be the will action. All the knowledge we may acquire can be used by the will in planning and carrying out its purposes. Knowledge, therefore, derived from all sources, is a *means* used by the will, and increases the possibilities of its action.

But, secondly, there are found still more immediate means of stimulating and strengthening the will, namely, in the *feelings*. The feelings are more closely related to will than knowledge, at least in the sense of cause and effect. There is a gradual transition from the feelings up to will, as follows: interest in an object, inclination, desire and purpose, or will to secure it. We might say that will is only the final link in the chain, and the feelings and desires lead up to and produce the act of willing. Even will itself has been called a feeling by some psychologists and classed with the feelings. But the thing in which we are now most concerned is how to reach and strengthen the will through the feelings. Some of the feelings which powerfully influence the will are desire of approbation, ambition, love of knowledge, appreciation of the beautiful and the good; or, on the other side, rivalry, envy, hate, and ill-will. Now, it is clear that a cultivation of the feelings and emotions is possible which may strongly influence the purposes and decisions of the will, either in the right or wrong direction. It is just at this point that education is capable of a vigorous influence in moulding the character of a child. The cultivation of the *six interests* already mentioned is little else than a cultivation of the great classes of feeling, for interest always contains a strong element of feeling. It is certain in any case that a child's, and eventually a man's will, is to be guided largely by his feelings. Whether any *care is taken* in education or not, feeling, good or bad, is destined to guide the will. Most people, as we know, are too much influenced by their feelings. This is apparent in the adage, "Think twice before you speak." Feelings of malice and ill-will, of revenge and envy, of dislike and jealously, get the control in many lives, because they have been permitted to grow and nothing better has been put in their place. The teacher by *selecting the proper materials* of study is able to cultivate and strengthen such feelings as sympathy and kindliness toward others; appreciation of brave, unselfish acts in others; the feeling of generosity, charity, and a forgiving spirit; a love for honesty and uprightness; a desire and ambition for knowledge in many directions. On the other hand, the teacher may gently instill a *dislike* for cowardice, meanness, selfishness, laziness, and envy, and bring the child to master and control these evil dispositions. Not only is it possible to cultivate those feelings which we may summarize as the love of the virtues and develop a dislike and turning away from vices, but this work of cultivating the feelings may be carried on so systematically that great *habits* of feeling are formed, and these habits become the very strongholds of character. They are the forces acting upon the will and guiding its choice.

It is *freedom of the will* to chose the best that we are after. We desire to limit the choice of the will if possible to good things. We desire to make the character so strong and so noble and consistent in its desires that it will not be strongly tempted by evil. The will in the end, while it controls all the life and action, is itself under the guidance of those *habits* of thought and feeling that have been gradually formed. Sully says, "Thus it is feeling that ultimately supplies the stimulus or force to volition and intellect which guides or illumines it."

A study of the will in its relation to knowledge and feeling reveals that the training and development of the will depend upon *exercise* and upon *instruction*. There are two ways of exercising will power. First, by requiring it to obey authority promptly and to control the body and the mind at the direction of another. The discipline of a school may exert a strong influence upon pupils in teaching them concentration and will power under the direction of another. Especially is this true in lower grades. Children in the first grade have but little power or habit of concentrating the attention. The will of the teacher, combined with her tact, must aid in developing the energies of the will in these little ones. The primary value of quick obedience in school, of exact discipline in marching, rising, etc., is twofold. It secures the necessary orderliness and it trains the will. Even in higher and normal schools such a perfect discipline has a great value in training to alertness and quickness of apprehension associated with action.

Secondly, by the training of the mind to freedom of action, to *self-activity*, to independence. As soon as children begin to develop the power of thought and action their self-activity should be encouraged. Even in the lowest grades the beginnings may be made. An *aim* may be set before them which they are to reach by their own efforts. For example, let a class in the first reader be asked to make a list of all the words in the last two lessons containing *th*, or *oi*, or some other combination. *Activity* rather than repose is the nature of children, and even in the kindergarten this activity is directed to the attainment of definite ends. With number work in the first grade the objects should be handled by the children, the letters made, rude drawings sketched, so as to give play to their active powers as well as to lead them on to confidence in doing, to an increase of self-activity. As children grow older, the problems set before them, the aims held out, should be more difficult. Of course they should be of *interest* to the child, so that it will have an impulse and desire of its own to reach them.

There are few things so valuable as setting up *definite aims* before children and then supplying them with incentives to reach them through their own efforts. It has been often supposed that the only way to do this is to use *reference books*, to study up the lesson or some topics of it outside of the regular order. But self-activity is by no means limited to such outside work. A child's self-activity may be often aroused by the manner of studying a simple lesson from a text-book. When a reading or geography lesson is so studied that the pupil thoroughly sifts the piece, hunts down the thought till he is certain of its meaning; when all the previous knowledge the pupil can command is brought to bear upon this, to throw light upon it; when the dictionary and any other books familiar to the child are studied for the sake of reference and explanation, self-activity is developed. Whenever the disposition can be stimulated to look at a fact or statement from *more than one standpoint*, to *criticise* it even, to see how true it is, or if there are exceptions, self-activity is cultivated.

The pursuit of definite aims always calls out the will and their satisfactory attainment strengthens one's confidence in his ability to succeed. Every step should be toward a clearly seen aim. At least this is our ideal in working with children. They should not be led on blindly from one point to another, but try to reach definite results.

There is a gradual *transition* in the course of a child's schooling from training of the will under guidance to its independent exercise. Throughout the school course there must be much obedience and will effort under the guidance of one in authority. But there should be a gradual increase of self-activity and self-determination. When the pupil leaves school he should be prepared to launch out and pursue his own aims with success.

Will effort, however, to be valuable, must have its roots in those *moral convictions* which it is the chief aim of the school to foster and strengthen. We have attempted to show in the preceding chapters how the central subject matter of the school could be chosen, and the other studies concentrated about it with a view to accomplishing this result. In concluding our discussion of general principles of education, and in summing up the results, basing our reasoning upon psychology, we are always forced to the conclusion that education aims at the *will*, and more particularly at the will as influenced and guided by moral ideas. This is the same as saying that we have completed the circle and come around to our starting point, that *moral character is the chief aim of education*.

Teachers who are interested in this phase of pedagogy will do well to study the *science of ethics*. Not that it will much aid them directly in school work, but it will at least give them a more comprehensive and definite notion of the field of morals and perhaps indicate more clearly where the *materials* of moral education are to be sought, and the leading ideas to be emphasized.

Herbart projected a system of ethics, based on psychology, with the intention of classifying the chief moral notions and of showing their relation to each other. He also developed a theory of the *origin* of moral ideas and their best means of cultivation, and then based his system of pedagogy upon it.

The chief classes of ethical ideas of Herbart are briefly explained as follows:

1. *Good will*. It is manifested in the sympathy we feel for the sorrow or joy of another person. It is illustrated by the example of Sidney and Howard already cited.

2. *Legal right*. It serves to avoid strife by some agreement or established rule; *e.g.*, the government of the United States fixes the law for pre-empting land and for homestead claims so that no two persons can lay claim to the same piece of land.

3. *Justice*, as expressed by reward or punishment. When a person purposely does an injury to another, all men unite in the judgment, "He must be punished." Likewise, if a kind act is done to anyone, we insist upon a return of gratitude at

least.

4. *Perfection of will.* This implies that the will is strong enough to resist all opposition. David's will to go out and meet Goliath was perfect. A boy desires to get his lesson, but indolence and the love of play are too strong for his will. There is nothing which goes so far to make up the character of the hero as strength of will which yields to no difficulties.

5. *Inner freedom.* This is the obedience of the will to its *highest* moral incentive. It is ability to set the will free from all selfish or wrong desires and to yield implicit obedience to moral ideas. This of course depends upon the cultivation of the other ideas and their proper subordination, one to another.

The five moral ideas just given indicate the lines along which strength of moral character is shown. They are of some interest to the teacher as a systematic arrangement of morals, but they are of no direct value in teaching. They are the most abstract and general classes of moral ideas and are of no interest whatever to children.

In morals the only thing that interests children is *moral action.* Whether it be in actual life or in a story or history, the child is aroused by a deed of kindness or courage. But all talk of kindness or goodness in general, disconnected from particular persons and actions, is dry and uninteresting. This gives us *the key to the child's* mind in morals. Not moralizing, not preaching, not lecturing, not reproof, can ever be the *original source* of moral ideas with the young, but the *actions* of people they see, and of those about whom they read or hear. Moral judgments and feelings spring up originally only in connection with human action in the concrete. If we propose then to *adapt moral teaching* to youthful minds, we must make use of concrete materials, observations of people taken from what the children have seen, stories and biographies of historical characters. A story of a man's life is interesting because it brings out his particular motives and actions. This is the field in which instruction has its conquests to make over youthful minds.

We will gather up the fruits of our discussion in the preceding chapters. Having fixed the chief aim in the effort to influence and strengthen moral character, we find *concentration* to be the central principle in which all others unite. It is the focusing of life and school experiences in the unity of the personality. The worth and choice of studies is determined by this. Interest unites knowledge, feeling, and will. The culture epochs supply the nucleus of materials for moral-educative purposes. Apperception assimilates new ideas by bringing each into the bond of its kindred and friends, spinning threads of connection in every direction. The inductive process collects, classifies, and organizes knowledge, everywhere tending toward unity.

CHAPTER VIII.

HERBART AND HIS DISCIPLES.

"Then, only, can a person be said to draw education under his control, when he has the wisdom to bring forth in the youthful soul a great circle or body of ideas, well knit together in its inmost parts—a body of ideas which is able to outweigh what is unfavorable in environment and to absorb and combine with itself the favorable elements of the same." (Herbart.)

Herbart was an empirical psychologist, and believed that the mind grows with what it feeds upon; that is, that it develops its powers slowly by experience. We are dependent not only upon our habits, upon the established trends of mental action produced by exercise and discipline, but also upon our acquired ideas, upon the thought materials stored up and organized in the mind. These thought-materials seem to possess a kind of vitality, an energy, an attractive or repulsive power. When ideas once gain real significance in the mind, they become active agents. They are not the blocks with which the mind builds. They are a part of the mind itself. They are the conscious reaction of the mind upon external things. The conscious ego itself is a product of experience. In thus referring all mental action and growth to experience, in the narrow limits he draws for the original powers of the mind, Herbart stands opposed to the older and to many more recent psychologists. He has been called the father of empirical psychology.

Kant, with many other psychologists, gives greater prominence to the original powers of the mind, to the *innate ideas,* by means of which it receives and works over the crude materials furnished by the senses. The difference between Kant and Herbart in interpreting the process of apperception is an index of a radical difference in their pedagogical standpoints. With Kant, apperception is the assimilation of the raw materials of knowledge through the fundamental categories of thought (quality, quantity, relation, modality, etc.) Kant's categories of thought are original properties of the mind; they receive the crude materials of sense-perception and give them form and meaning. With Herbart, the ideas gained through experience are the apperceiving power in interpreting new things. Practically, the difference between Kant and Herbart is important. For Kant gives controlling influence to innate ideas in the process of acquisition. Our capacity for learning depends not so much upon the results of experience and thought stored in the mind, as upon original powers, unaided and unsupported by experience. With Herbart, on the contrary, great stress is laid upon the *acquired fund* of empirical knowledge as a means of increasing one's stores, of more rapidly receiving and assimilating new ideas.

Upon this is also based psychologically the whole educational plan of Herbart and of his disciples. As fast as ideas are gained they are used as means of further acquisition. The chief care is to supply the mind of a child at any stage of his growth with materials of knowledge suited to his previous stores, and to see that the new is properly assimilated by the old and organized with it. This accumulated fund of ideas, as it goes on collecting and arranging itself in the mind, is not only a favorable condition but an active agency in our future acquisition and progress. Moreover, it is the business of the teacher to guide and, to some extent, to control the inflow of new ideas and experiences into the mind of a child; to superintend the process of acquiring and of building up those bodies of thought and feeling which eventually are to influence and guide a child's voluntary action.

The critics therefore accuse Herbart of a sort of *architectural* design or even of a *mechanical* process in education. If our ability and character depend to such an extent upon our acquirements, and if the teacher is able to control the supply of ideas to a child and to guide the process of arrangement, he can build up controlling centers of thought which may strongly influence the action of the will. In other words, he can construct a character by building the right materials into it. This seems to leave small room for spontaneous development toward self-activity and freedom.

Herbart, on the other hand, criticises Kant's idea of the transcendental freedom of the will, on the ground that, if true, it makes deliberate, systematic education impossible. If the will remains absolutely free in spite of acquired knowledge, in spite of strongly developed tendencies of thought and feeling; if the child or youth, at any moment, even in later years, is able to retire into his trancendental *ego* and arrive at decisions without regard to the effect of previously acquired ideas and habits, any well-planned, intentional effort at education is empty and without effect.

John Friedrich Herbart, the founder of this movement in education, was born at Oldenburg in 1776, and died at Göttingen in 1841. He labored seven years at Göttingen at the beginning of his career as professor, and a similar period at its close. But the longest period of his university teaching was at Königsberg, where, for twenty-five years, he occupied the chair of philosophy made famous before him by Kant. His writings and lectures were devoted chiefly to philosophy, psychology, and pedagogy. Previous to beginning his career as professor at the university, he had spent three years as private tutor to three boys in a Swiss family of patrician rank. In the letters and reports made to the father of these boys, we have strong proof of the practical wisdom and earnestness with which he met his duties as a teacher. The deep pedagogical interest thus developed in him remained throughout his life a quickening influence. One of his earliest courses of lectures at the university resulted in the publication, in 1806, of his Allgemeine Pädagogik, his leading work on education, and to-day one of the classics of German educational literature. His vigorous philosophical thinking in psychology and ethics gave him the firm basis for his pedagogical system. At Königsberg, so strong was his interest in educational problems that he established a training-school for boys, where teachers, chosen by him and under his direction, could make practical application of his decided views on education. Though small, this school continued to furnish proof of the correctness of his educational ideas till he left Königsberg in 1833. This, we believe, was the first practice-school of its kind established in connection with pedagogical lectures in any German university. It should be remembered that, while Herbart was a philosopher of the first rank, even among the eminent thinkers of Germany and of the world, he attested his profound interest in education, not only by systematic lectures and extensive writings on education, but by maintaining for nearly a quarter of a century a practice-school at the university, for the purpose of testing and illustrating his educational convictions. Lectures on pedagogy are more or less common-place, and often nearly worthless. The lecturer on pedagogy who shuns the life of the school room is not half a man in his profession. The example thus set by Herbart of bringing the maturest fruit of philosophical study into the school room, and testing it day by day and month by month upon children has been followed by several eminent disciples of Herbart at important universities.

Karl Volkmar Stoy (1815-1885) in 1843 began his career of more than forty years as professor of pedagogy and leader of a teachers' seminary and practice-school at Jena. (A part of this time was spent at Heidelberg.) During these years more than six hundred university students received a spirited introduction to the theory and practice of education under Stoy's guidance and inspiration. His seminary for discussion and his practice-school became famous throughout Germany and sent out many men who gained eminence in educational labors.

Tuiskon Ziller, in 1862, set up at Leipzig, in connection with his lectures on teaching, a pedagogical seminary and practice-school, which, for twenty years, continued to develop and extend the application of Herbart's ideas. Ziller and several of his disciples have attained much prominence as educational writers and leaders.

A year after the death of Stoy, 1886, Dr. Wilhelm Rein was called to the chair of pedagogy at Jena. He had studied both with Stoy and Ziller, and had added to this an extensive experience as a teacher and as principal of a normal school. His lectures on pedagogy, both theoretical and practical, in connection with his seminary for discussion and his practice-school for application of theory, furnish an admirable introduction to the most progressive educational ideas of Germany.

The Herbart school stands for certain progressive ideas which, while not exactly new, have, however, received such a new infusion of life-giving blood that the vague formulæ of theorists have been changed into the definite, mandatory requirements and suggestions of real teachers. The fact that a pedagogical truth has been vaguely or even clearly stated a dozen times by prominent writers, is no reason for supposing that it has ever had any vital influence upon educators. The history of education shows conclusively that important educational ideas can be written about and talked about for centuries without finding their way to any great extent into school rooms. What we now need in education is definite and well-grounded theories and plans, backed up by honest and practical execution.

The Herbartians have patiently submitted themselves to thorough-going tests in both theory and practice. After years of experiment and discussion, they come forward with certain propositions of reform which are designed to infuse new life and meaning into educational labors.

The first proposition is to make the foundation of education immovable by resting it upon *growth in moral character*, as the purpose which serious teachers must put first. The selection of studies and the organization of the school course follow this guiding principle.

The second is *permanent, many-sided interest*. The life-giving power which springs from the awakening of the best interests in the two great realms of real knowledge should be felt by every teacher. Though not entirely new, this idea is better than new, because its deeper meaning is clearly brought out, and it is rationally provided for by the selection of interesting materials and by marking out an appropriate method of treatment. All knowledge must be infused with feelings of interest, if it is to reach the heart and work its influence upon character by giving impulse to the will.

Thirdly, the idea of *organized unity*, or concentration, in the mental stores gathered by children, in all their knowledge and experience, is a thought of such vital meaning in the effort to establish unity of character, that, when a teacher once realizes its import, his effort is toned up to great undertakings.

Fourthly, the *culture epochs* give a suggestive bird's-eye view of the historical meaning of education, and of the rich materials of history and literature for supplying suitable mental food to children. They help to realize the ideas of interest, concentration, and apperception.

Apperception is the practical key to the most important problems of education, because it compels us to keep a sympathetic eye upon the child in his moods, mental states, and changing phases of growth; to build hourly upon the only foundation he has, his previous acquirements and habits.

Finally, the Herbartians have grappled seriously with that great and comprehensive problem *the common school course*. The obligation rests upon them to select the materials and to lay out a course of study which embodies all their leading principles in a form suited to children and to our school conditions.

Some of the principal books published in English bearing on Herbart are as follows:

De Garmo, Charles. Essentials of Method. D. C. Heath, Boston.

Felkin. The Science of Education; a translation of some of Herbart's most important writings on education, with a short biography of Herbart. D. C. Heath & Co., Boston.

Lange. Ueber Apperception, translated by the Herbart Club and edited by Dr. De Garmo. D. C. Heath & Co., Boston.

Lindner's Psychology, translated by Dr. De Garmo. D. C. Heath & Co., Boston.

Smith, Miss M. K. Herbart's Psychology, translated. International Ed. series. Appleton.

Van Liew. Outlines of Pedagogics, by Rein and Van Liew. C. W. Bardeen, Syracuse, N. Y.

The latter book contains a full bibliography of the German works of the Herbart school as well as of those thus far published in English.

Printed by Libri Plureos GmbH in Hamburg,
Germany